VILLAGES
OF ENGLAND

The Gilbert White memorial window at Selborne, Hampshire, showing St Francis and friends in the village.

VILLAGES OF ENGLAND

BRIAN BAILEY

HARMONY BOOKS

NEW YORK

Published in the United States in 1984 by Harmony Books, a division of Crown Publishers, Inc., One Park Avenue, New York, New York 10016

Published originally in Great Britain in 1984 by George Weidenfeld & Nicolson Limited, 91 Clapham High Street, London SW4 7TA

HARMONY and colophon are trademarks of Crown Publishers, Inc.

Manufactured in Italy

Library of Congress Cataloging in Publication Data

Bailey, Brian J.
   Villages of England.

   Includes index.
    1. England—Description and travel—1971–   —Guide-books. 2. England—History, Local. 3. Villages—England—Guide-books. I. Title.
DA650.B23 1984   914.2′04857   83–22824
ISBN 0–517–55343–0

10 9 8 7 6 5 4 3 2 1

First American Edition

CONTENTS

INTRODUCTION

THERE are those who say that the English village is done for – that it's an outmoded form of community in an urbanised and technological world. But that is clearly untrue. The village is merely changing its nature again as it has done before. The traditional English village, with its nucleus of church and village green, shop and pub, smithy, rectory and school, with manor house and farmhouses at the fringes, and houses and tied cottages in between – housing chiefly farm labourers or workers on the squire's estate – is taking on a different kind of community identity. The church is now frequently locked against vandals; there is no resident parson; the school and the smithy have long since gone; the shop is a self-service mini-market; and the squire, if he still exists, is so far from ruling the roost in temporal matters as the parson in spiritual ones, that he is grateful nowadays to be invited to judge the best dahlias at the annual flower show. The old lover's lane, where generations of villagers did their courting, has been built up with smart new bungalows to house the young executives who live here in

The changing village scene. Alfriston, Sussex, as it was in 1910, with the Star Inn on the left – the lack of traffic and tourists seems uncanny.

The more familiar view of Alfriston today, showing the Star Inn with its timber-framing revealed. The village is busier but still full of character.

place of the farmworkers (who now ironically reside on town council estates). It is lined at evenings and weekends with company cars which far outnumber tractors and farm wagons, outside cottages with aluminium double glazing, and the village's most glittering new business is the petrol filling station built on the site of the former blacksmith's forge.

But for all that, the village is still a small rural settlement highly characteristic of the English nation, and the people who live in it are generally in voluntary communion with the quiet countryside rather than the concrete jungle. Our villages are living entities, not museums, and sighs of love, shrieks of childbirth and shouts of joy are still its echoes as they always were. There may be more television aerials on the roofs than headstones in the churchyard, but the cycle of life goes on as before, and though it is no longer the close community thriving on agriculture and mutual trust that it once was, the English village is still an essential symbol of

the English character: an institution that does not extend to anything like the same extent into Wales or Scotland. Even as you drive towards villages in different parts of the country (for 'seeing the countryside' is now done by car rather than by foot, bicycle or horse) you can observe by the road signs how nature and local preoccupations have formed the kind of village you are approaching. In the south west, for instance, you may find 'Bends for 3 miles' more often than in the Chilterns, where 'Single track road with passing places' is more likely. The 'Gated road' between villages in Leicestershire will probably be 'Road liable to subsidence' in mining areas of the north Midlands; whilst in the Pennines and Cumbria 'Steep hill, 1 in 4' is a common introduction to your village destination. But let us pass from the general to the particular, for whilst all big towns are the same, no two villages are alike, and this is an important part of their eternal charm.

The Garden of England. A characteristic Kentish scene at Crouch, with spring blossom framing the traditional kilns or oast houses in which hops were dried for making ale.

LONDON AND THE SOUTH-EAST

MOST visitors to this country from abroad arrive via London or the south east ports, and their first impressions of England come from flying over or motoring through the Kentish landscape, the Garden of England. This is as good a place as any to start our tour of English villages, for wherever we begin, what we find there will not be typical of the whole country. One of the virtues of the 13000 or more villages of England (I take the figure on trust) is their enormous variety. They have a diversity of size, of style and of situation that paradoxically unites them, and this common quality distinguishes them as epitomes of an England which has changed relatively little over a period of a thousand years.

This may be hard to accept when we see villages on the main roads to London, with heavy traffic thundering through what were once quiet village streets; or when we stand in a city suburb which was once a sleepy village in the fields, now consumed by twentieth-century urban expansion. But these villages, victims of our industrial age, are not typical either, and we never have far to go before we escape the noise and rush and come upon quieter and more picturesque places that represent the older, more

Croydon, Surrey. An engraving showing Croydon – now the county's largest town and part of Greater London – when it was no more than a large village, surrounded by fields.

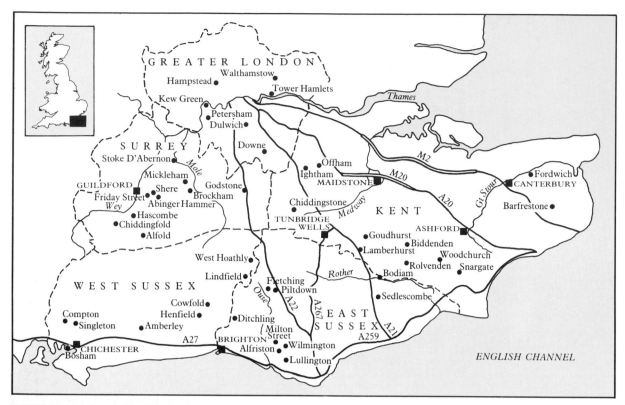

Barfrestone, Kent. The south door of the church of St Nicholas, surrounded by walls of flint and Caen stone, displays sumptuous Norman carving of beasts and men.

traditional way of life which is still an important part of our national character. For nearly every real Englishman (or, at any rate, every Englishwoman) dreams of a little cottage in the country, with roses growing round the door and the scent of honeysuckle drifting in from the garden.

Hardly more than a couple of miles off the Dover road to Canterbury is **Barfrestone**, where the church bell resides in a little wooden cote built into a yew tree. But to assume that the church was too poor to have a belfry would be a mistake for it is a Norman building with an amazing richness of carving. The bell, in fact, calling the faithful to worship from its muffling evergreen canopy, aptly symbolises the charm and eccentricity of much of rural England, whilst the church itself provides interesting evidence of something else that will feature largely throughout our travels – building materials.

Barfrestone's church is built of flint and Caen stone. Flint is the only readily available building stone in this chalky region of England, but it is difficult to work, and when the Norman invaders began to replace the mainly timber churches of the Anglo-Saxons, they found it expedient to ship stone across the Channel from their own homeland rather

Romney Marsh. A view near Snargate of the area recovered from the sea by drainage operations to produce highly fertile farmland where villages are few and sheep many.

than drag stone across country from English quarries farther west. So in the villages of the south east, there is a considerable mixture of materials – flint and stone, timber and brick.

Fordwich, to the north west, was once a river port on the Stour where Norman vessels unloaded Caen stone for Canterbury Cathedral. An ancient crane can still be seen there. Fordwich also has an old town hall, sometimes said to be the smallest in England, built of brick and timber in the time of Henry VIII. This anomaly provides another point of interest concerning English villages – they were not necessarily always villages. Many places which are unquestionably villages now have declined from being small towns, while others, for various reasons, have disappeared altogether.

Snargate is a case in point. It is a tiny hamlet on the area of flat land reclaimed from the sea, known as Romney Marsh, where men are outnumbered by sheep, frogs and wildfowl. William Cobbett called it 'a village with five houses and with a church capable of containing two thousand people'. Clearly Snargate has shrunk in size since the church was built, probably as a result of population movement due to changing fortunes, as the nature of this misty marshland was much altered by drainage and the silting up of streams. Richard Barham, author of the *Ingoldsby Legends*, was rector here, and wrote that the world is divided into five parts, 'namely Europe, Asia, Africa, America and Romney Marsh.' Certainly the smugglers here were a strange lot, for they carried on their illicit business without troubling to avoid Mr Barham, saying 'it's only parson' as he passed by.

The Biddenden Maids. This Kentish village sign shows the legendary Siamese twins who were joined at the hips and inaugurated a charity for the local poor each Easter.

Woodchurch is a large village with a triangular green at its centre. It has a fine Early English church (built of stone despite the name), a windmill and several characteristic Wealden hall-houses. Names can provide valuable clues to the histories of different parts of England. Farther west, Kentish villages such as **Rolvenden** and **Biddenden** show their Anglo-Saxon origins in the 'den' ending, which signifies a place in a wooded valley, or a clearance for pasturing animals. Farther north, mainly in the east, the Danish 'by' ending appears in villages founded during the ninth and tenth centuries. Cornish villages are frequently named after Celtic saints, while 'Ends' and 'Greens' are common in Hertfordshire, but not in Cumbria, where harsher Viking accents prevail.

Rolvenden is well known for its restored windmill, but less familiar is the sometime home of Frances Burnett, the novelist nicknamed 'Fluffy' whose most enduring work was *Little Lord Fauntleroy*. It seems that she was never sure whether she preferred England or America, but during one of her stays here she lived at Great Maytham Hall, now converted into flats.

The famous Maids, shown on the Biddenden village sign, were Siamese twins who, according to legend, started a local charity by giving bread and cheese to poor old folk at Easter. The villages of the Weald became important centres of Flemish weaving at one time, and half-timbered weavers' houses line Biddenden's High Street, where there is also a fine gabled and tile-hung Cloth Hall.

Lamberhurst also retains much of its old character, and has the additional attraction of Scotney Old Castle, a ruined medieval tower and manor house surrounded by a picturesque moat. The so-called Owl House in the village was a wool-smugglers' haunt – smugglers were known as 'owlers' in these parts once. One notorious group of eighteenth-century smugglers known as the Hawkhurst Gang had one of their bases at the Star and Eagle in the lovely hilltop village of **Goudhurst,** and the villagers caught and hanged the gangleader on the nearby heath in 1796.

Even as one gets perilously close to London, Kent still has its village delights. **Chiddingstone**, near Tonbridge, is now in the care of the National Trust. Legend has it that the name comes from a large rock called the Chiding Stone, where nagging medieval wives were given a dose of their own medicine by the assembled village population. This is a single street village, with fine half-timbered houses built with profits from the once-thriving Wealden iron industry.

Ightham is another fine village, best known for Ightham Mote, a well-preserved medieval manor house outside the village, with swans on its moat. The village itself is worth pausing in, for its main street has Tudor shops and houses, and its churchyard has examples of a curious local speciality – headstones shaped like human heads and shoulders with macabre death's heads carved on their hoodmoulds.

Offham, nearby, is unique in that it sports a quintain on its green. The quintain was a target used in medieval tilting or jousting practice. A valiant knight would ride 'full tilt' at it, but his squire – an inexperienced apprentice – might be knocked off his horse as the pivoted arm swung round and hit him with the sandbag on the other end. Quintain practice was thus good fun for spectators, but it also trained good horsemen and lancers for more serious purposes. On this western side of the Medway, Kentish Men are subtly distinguished from Men of Kent, across the river, in one of those ancient concentrations of local as opposed to national pride which persist in much of rural England.

Fordwich, Kent. The town hall, with – alas – the town stocks reverently preserved outside, was built in the sixteenth century and is said to be England's smallest.

Scotney Old Castle, Kent. A romantic building near Lamberhurst, the 'castle' is a seventeenth-century manor house built on to a medieval tower and surrounded by a moat.

Anne of Cleves House, Ditchling. Several Tudor houses in England have the same name as this Sussex building, and it is doubtful if the queen had anything to do with this one.

Crossing over from the county of oast-houses and spring blossom into East Sussex, we find villages of tile-hung and weatherboarded cottages nestling beneath the chalk downs, where skylarks sing high above the grazing sheep. Near the village of **Bodiam**, as well as its famous castle ruins surrounded by a lily-laden moat, is the largest hop farm in Britain, for Kent is not the only county where hops are grown for making the ale consumed in village pubs from one end of the country to the other.

Sedlescombe is an attractive village a few miles to the south, with a long triangular green bearing the old village pump. A large number of Anglo-Saxon coins was discovered here in the nineteenth century, and is said to have been secreted by King Harold's treasurer after the Battle of Hastings.

Chiddingstone, Kent. A fine street village of stylish half-timbered houses, dating from the sixteenth and seventeenth centuries, it is preserved by the National Trust.

Ightham Mote, Kent. A combination of stone and timber-framed building, this romantic medieval manor house near Sevenoaks was once owned by Richard Haut, Sheriff of Kent.

The enigmatic Long Man of Wilmington, from a woodcut by Leslie Ward. Theories about its origins abound but the mystery remains unsolved.

Down towards the coast where the South Downs halt abruptly in towering chalk cliffs above Eastbourne, Alfriston and Lullington nestle close together in the valley of the Cuckmere River. Alf-**riston** is a popular village always crowded in the summer months. Its fifteenth-century Star inn on the village street sports the figurehead of a Dutch ship wrecked in the English Channel in the seventeenth century. The church of St Andrew stands somewhat isolated from the village across a meadow and it is called the 'Cathedral of the Downs'.

Lullington, in contrast, is notable for one of England's smallest churches, while **Wilmington**, not far away, is famous for one of the world's largest human images, cut in the turf of a chalk hillside, standing 226 feet (68.7 m) high, and known as the Wilmington Long Man. No one knows his age, but he may have been cut in Anglo-Saxon times.

Piltdown, East Sussex. The fellow on the village inn sign, who is not as old as he looks, reminds us that a nod is as good as a wink to a gullible anthropologist.

Another member of this little group is **Milton Street**, a hamlet less invaded by tourists but occupying a preciously quiet position on the downs. It was the unlikely location – at first sight – of another find of Anglo-Saxon coins, but this is the area where the continental invaders first established themselves on this island.

Ditchling, near the border with West Sussex, is an ideal village for walkers. Ditchling Beacon, nearby, is one of the highest points on the South Downs, and the landscape is always dotted with the white spots which are the renowned Downland sheep. The village boasts an ancient house which may have belonged to Henry VIII's fourth wife. Ditchling's link with Anne of Cleves is not so strong as its connection with modern English artists and

Afriston, East Sussex. This fearsome character outside the fifteenth-century Star Inn is a Dutch ship's figurehead – one among many interesting features of the village.

craftsmen, which dates from a Bohemian colony set up here in the twenties by a group including Eric Gill and Frank Brangwyn.

In medieval times, arrowheads for the king's archers were made in these parts, and **Fletching**'s name undoubtedly comes from the French for arrow, *fléche*. The great historian of the Roman empire, Edward Gibbon, is buried in the parish church, but the district's other supposed associations with ancient history will not be allowed to rest in peace for a long time yet, for the hamlet of **Piltdown**, nearby, is notorious for the so-called Piltdown Skull, said by excited archaeologists after its discovery in 1912 to be a human skull from the Pleistocene period of prehistory, but exposed in 1953 as a fake. The village pub has profited from the hoax if no one else.

The Cat House, Henfield. This image, repeated round the walls, has added to Henfield's surfeit of zoological names. There is also an Ants Manor in this West Sussex village.

Just across the border into West Sussex is **Lindfield**, with a highly picturesque tree-lined High Street of Tudor and Georgian buildings. It has been called 'without any doubt the finest village street in East Sussex', but recent boundary changes have made that tribute redundant, by switching it to the western county along with **West Hoathly**, which stands on a hilltop at the edge of Ashdown Forest. The church mice of St Margaret's, West Hoathly, must be wary of the Cat Inn close by, but a bird was the victim at the large village of **Henfield**. It seems that an old lady living in a little thatched cottage there had a canary which fell victim to the vicar's cat. The distressed lady hanged an effigy of the cat at her door which has since been replaced by a whole troop of black cats with birds in their paws, silhouetted round the walls of what became known as the Cat House.

Larger mammals obviously account for the name of **Cowfold**, a village exquisite at its centre, with brick-built and weatherboarded cottages grouped prettily round the churchyard. St Peter's contains a memorial to Thomas Nelond, a prior of Lewes, in the form of an elaborate brass, ten feet (3 m) long, with a life-size image of the prior.

Amberley is one of the showplace villages of Sussex. It is well preserved and contains a 'castle' besides a wealth of the assorted building materials familiar in this region. Amberley Castle was actually a well fortified medieval manor house belonging to the Bishop of Chichester, with a two-storey lodging or barrack block for the Bishop's private army. It is in ruins now, and makes an attractive group with the Norman village church beside it. An aspect of the village more characteristic of this part of England is the mixture of timber, flint, brick and clunch (chalk) in the village houses, which with their roofs of thatch or tile, all have a very neat and well cared-for appearance.

If it were not for the difference in building materials, you could almost mistake **Bosham** for a Cornish coastal village, but its brick, flint and tiles betray its Sussex identity. It is a quaint place popular with yachtsmen, built on a peninsula projecting out into Chichester Harbour. It was here that the great Dane, Cnut or Canute, is supposed to have made his effective little demonstration of the limits of kingly power by ordering the incoming tide to go back, and a daughter of the king is said to be buried in the churchyard.

Brick, flint and tiles also go to make up the cottages at **Compton**, a largish village for these parts on the chalk downs. H. G. Wells spent some time here in his younger days, and said that the place 'had a great effect on me'.

Singleton has cottages of flint spread out along the lanes around its pretty duckpond and is the image of English rural peace. It preserves relics of an England not yet entirely lost, in the Weald and Downland Museum, an open-air site where interesting old buildings under threat of demolition have been carefully reassembled after skilful dismantling, as well as exhibits from the former iron industry of the Sussex Weald.

Moving northward into the well-wooded county of Surrey, a distinct change in the style of the villages is evident. Instead of a predominance of 'street' villages, stretched out along old country roads – now, alas, sometimes transformed into

Singleton, West Sussex. The duckpond of an attractive and well-kept village which boasts the fascinating Weald and Downland open-air museum of old buildings and industry.

major inter-city highways – we have almost a surfeit of 'green' villages, for Surrey has more village greens than any other county of England.

Brockham has one of the best village greens. It is of the classic triangular shape overlooked by the church (which is actually modern but looks ancient), and surrounded by shady trees where village cricket matches can be enjoyed on summer weekends. It would take a whole book to explain this uniquely English institution to anyone for whom cricket is a foreign eccentricity, but connoisseurs will tell you in hushed tones of reverence that W.G.Grace once batted on the green at Brockham. The crack of bat on ball is probably the noisiest thing to disturb the serenity of this sunny village beside the River Mole, despite its alarming closeness to the spreading metropolis. In winter, however, the green takes on a different aspect, when its annual bonfire is lit on Guy Fawkes night.

At **Abinger Hammer**, where the figure of a blacksmith strikes the passing hours on the village clock, another custom that has survived the onslaughts of narrow-minded bigots takes place on May Day, when children dance round a garlanded maypole in a pagan ritual to celebrate spring fertility. The Puritans called the maypole a 'stinckying idoll' and banned its use, cutting down those maypoles that were erected permanently on England's village greens. But the people's memory was longer than the Puritan rule, and in due course the maypole returned to some places, such as Abinger, as a harmless expression of seasonal joy.

E.M.Forster lived at West Hackhurst, north of Abinger Hammer for many years, and gave Piney Copse, near his home, to the National Trust. Literary associations are also among the attractions of **Mickleham**, which is, for a change, a street village. Situated in the Mole valley, it has beautiful beech woods around it and the celebrated beauty spot Box Hill in the vicinity. The novelist Fanny Burney was married in the church (which has rare wooden grave-boards in its burial ground) as was

Brockham, Surrey. Cricket matches are now played elsewhere in this village,

but the traditional view of the game beneath the spire of Christ Church takes some beating.

George Meredith in the following century. Meredith lived in a cottage on Zigzag Hill, and at one period was to be seen daily being taken up to the top of Box Hill in a bath-chair drawn by his donkey, 'Picnic'. In Fanny Burney's time, refugees from revolutionary France came to Mickleham, including Talleyrand and Madame de Staël, and in the nineteenth century, writers visiting the village included Keats, Robert Louis Stevenson, Marie Corelli and Henry James.

Chiddingfold village green is not so obviously triangular as Brockham's, but it, too, is faced by the village church, and has a duckpond. The church has a lancet window containing carefully arranged fragments of coloured glass found in the vicinity, for the village was a medieval glass-making centre. The local craftsmen drank their ale in the Crown Inn 500 years ago, and it claims to be the oldest pub in the country. This boast should be treated with some scepticism, however, since there are almost as many contenders for this title as there are silver birches on the Surrey slopes.

Hascombe is a very attractive village, with houses built of stone, much tile-hanging, and some picturesque farmhouses. Generally speaking, however, Surrey is a place of delightful little surprise corners rather than whole beautiful villages. One such spot is at **Alfold**, where red tile-hung cottages line the approach to the village church, with its little broach spire, to create a very picturesque scene where modernism hardly intrudes at all, and **Shere** is another place of pretty corners. The names of villages and hamlets such as **Stoke d'Abernon** and **Friday Street** make them seem a million miles away from what is in reality a county largely overrun by London commuters. That Surrey can still show such unspoilt country retreats within twenty miles of Piccadilly Circus is a tribute to the enduring respect most Englishmen have for the thousand-year-old rural tradition of village life.

Godstone, for instance, manages to retain its village character within a stone's throw of Croydon and with the M25 motorway roaring by less than a mile away. It has a green with a duckpond, and

Abinger Hammer, Surrey. It is rather hard to see this joyful May Day celebration as a wicked pagan ritual, but it was banned by Cromwell's narrow-minded Puritans.

Alfold, Surrey. An exquisite corner typical of the best villages in Surrey, with brick and tile-hung cottages beside the footpath leading to the ancient village church.

village cricket is still played there in a setting of trees and village church, and its inn, the White Hart, which once won a rare compliment from William Cobbett for its flower garden.

Of course, resistance to urbanisation can never be totally successful. The growth of London is an irresistible force, and country villages are not, alas immovable objects. England's capital has crept out and swallowed up many a place that was once a sleepy rural village. The **Tower Hamlets** were so named because they were rural outposts beyond the Tower of London, the medieval city's eastern fortress defending London against attack from the Thames. Nowadays, however, one might easily imagine they take their name from the modern tower blocks that dominate the skyline. And little more than a century ago, **Walthamstow**, now a heavily built-up industrial suburb, was described as 'a drowsy village in the fields'.

Petersham and **Kew Green** are well inside Greater London but still retain a slightly superior villagey atmosphere in spite of the traffic – Kew Green, in particular, being frantically busy with the Royal Botanic Gardens at its threshold – and both places have some stylish houses. **Downe**, in Kent, is still a quiet village although it, too, is within the Greater London area. Down House was the home of Charles Darwin, one of the most influential and controversial Englishmen of modern times.

The old centres of one or two suburbs, such as **Dulwich** and **Hampstead**, still manage to retain a kind of village identity, but generally speaking, the once rural settlements around London are lost villages. They are as irretrievable now as those villages destroyed by the Black Death, despotic landowners or new reservoirs, and in our search for characteristic English villages we shall do well to move on elsewhere.

Avebury, Wiltshire. Bronze Age men erected the huge stone circle which practically engulfs the modern village, and many local buildings contain stone from the monoliths.

THE
SOUTH

TRAVELLING westward from the vicinity of London, the change in the kind of landscape is only gradual at first. The chalk familiar in Sussex continues through Hampshire into Dorset, and it is only half way across the latter county that a dramatic geological change is evident. Instead of the soft chalk and Tertiary rock that makes up most of Hampshire and the Isle of Wight, giving great white cliffs here and there along the coastline, Dorset reveals older and harder limestone rock. This influences not only the landscape, but also the style of the villages and, northward into Wiltshire, there are powerful reminders of the earliest settlers on this island.

To deal with Hampshire first, however, we have hardly crossed over from Surrey before we come upon **Selborne**, a village famous throughout the world as the home of Gilbert White, the parson-naturalist who died 15 years before Darwin was born. His grave is in the churchyard. White's *Natural History of Selborne* has become one of the most enduring of English books, and his house is now a well-attended museum devoted to White himself, and to Captain L.E.G.Oates, who died with Scott in Antarctica.

Gilbert White wrote that the high ground to the south east of Selborne consists of 'a vast hill of chalk rising 300 feet [91.2 m] above the village; and is

Selborne, Hampshire. This peaceful place was made famous by Gilbert White, who was the village parson by profession and the village naturalist and historian by partiality.

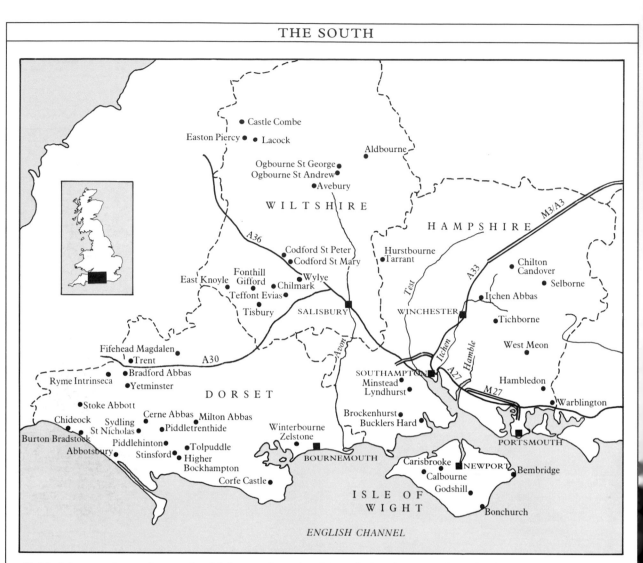

Castle Combe
Easton Piercy • Lacock
Aldbourne

Ogbourne St George
Ogbourne St Andrew
•Avebury

W I L T S H I R E

M3/A3

H A M P S H I R E

A36

Codford St Peter
Codford St Mary
Hurstbourne
Tarrant

Fonthill
Gifford
East Knoyle
Wylye
Chilmark
Chilton
Candover
Selborne

A33

Teffont Evias
Itchen Abbas

Tisbury
SALISBURY
WINCHESTER
Tichborne

West Meon

Fifehead Magdalen
•Trent
A30

Ryme Intrinseca
Bradford Abbas
•Yetminster

D O R S E T

Azon

Test

Itchen

Hamble

SOUTHAMPTON
Minstead
Lyndhurst
Hambledon

A27

M27

Stoke Abbott
Warblington

Chideock
Sydling
St Nicholas
Cerne Abbas
Milton Abbas
Brockenhurst
Bucklers Hard

Burton Bradstock
Piddlehinton
Piddletrenthide
Winterbourne
Zelstone

Abbotsbury
Stinsford
Higher
Bockhampton
Tolpuddle

PORTSMOUTH

Corfe Castle
BOURNEMOUTH

Carisbrooke
Calbourne
NEWPORT
Bembridge

Godshill

I S L E   O F
W I G H T

Bonchurch

ENGLISH CHANNEL

divided into a sheep down, the high wood, and a long hanging wood called the Hanger ...' This is a familiar chalk landscape, and **Buriton** is not dissimilar. Edward Gibbon was brought up in the manor house at the bottom of the hill with the downs and hanging woods likewise in view from the windows.

Villages go hand in hand with cricket in Hampshire, and two of the game's shrines are only six miles (9.6 km) apart, not far across the border from West Sussex. **Hambledon** and **West Meon** are both pretty villages in their own right, but mention of Hambledon stirs the blood of all true cricket enthusiasts, for what has been called (with justice) the finest team game ever invented by man was largely formulated by the Hambledon Club which played at Broadhalfpenny Down nearby. History and literature are practically silent about organised cricket until the Hambledon Club came

into being in 1760, but the inn where the players drank their ale is called the Bat and Ball, and stories of the club are legion. Perhaps the best of them for those who cannot abide the game itself concerns the caravan in which the players, scorer and umpire all travelled to away matches together. One day the caravan overturned on the road, and all the occupants clambered out except Peter Steward, known as 'Buck', who insisted that the others should put the vehicle upright with him inside it for, as he said, 'one good turn deserves another'. It was at the end of the Hambledon Club's greatest period that Thomas Lord (a Yorkshireman) founded Lord's cricket ground, the Mecca and El Dorado of modern cricket, and he is buried at West Meon.

Tichborne is an innocent-looking hamlet on the River Itchen near Winchester, but its name has become synonymous with two English eccentricities that are now part of national folklore: the

The Tichborne 'Crawl'. A Victorian engraving depicts Lady Mabella de Tichborne on her painful and fatal progress round twenty acres of land to establish a famous local charity.

'The Bat and Ball'. The inn at Hambledon perpetuates the memory of one of Hampshire's great gifts to civilised man – the establishment of cricket as an organised team game.

Tichborne Dole and the Tichborne Claimant. The Tichborne Dole was begun in the reign of Henry I by the lord of the manor's wife. She is said to have crawled round 20 acres (8.2 ha) of land, though fatally ill, to meet the challenge of her brutal husband, who offered her as much land as she could encompass in a given time to raise money for the poor of the village. Lady Mabella de Tichborne ought to be a greater national heroine than Lady Godiva, but to the English, riding naked through the streets is clearly a far more courageous act of heroism than mere self-sacrifice. However, the Tichborne Dole was thus established, and loaves of bread were given to the needy on 25 March each year. In 1871 the Claimant brought to the nation's notice a little village that no one had ever heard of before. An Australian butcher, Arthur Orton by name, claimed to be Sir Roger Tichborne, the rightful heir to the ancient family's estate, whom

Swan Green, Lyndhurst. The Verderers, who administer the New Forest laws, still meet in the court room of this Hampshire village known as the 'capital' of the forest.

everyone thought had been lost at sea. Orton had done his homework carefully, and a court case lasting three months and costing nearly £100,000 ensued, at the end of which Orton was declared an impostor and imprisoned for 14 years.

Hampshire possesses many villages with delightful double-barrelled names like **Itchen Abbas**, **Hurstbourne Tarrant** and **Chilton Candover**, usually close to a river or trickling stream which originally provided the first settlers with their water. The chalk streams remain unpolluted – many still provide fresh trout – and they are among the greatest delights of the Hampshire countryside, sometimes even supporting an ancient water-mill where for centuries the local farmers brought their wheat for grinding into flour.

The Test and Itchen rivers flow down to Southampton Water, which has on its west side the New Forest, where villages such as **Lyndhurst** and **Brockenhurst** still welcome the semi-wild ponies into their streets when traffic and visitors leave room for them. Some places in the Forest remain almost unbelievably quiet, however. I well remember walking from Lyndhurst to **Minstead** one Sunday morning some years ago, and sitting for an hour on the village green there with no sound except the intermittent drumming of a distant woodpecker to disturb the precious silence. In the churchyard of this peaceful place is the grave of Sir Arthur Conan Doyle.

Down the Beaulieu River toward the Solent is a village of a very different sort. **Bucklers Hard** was a shipbuilding centre, and its single very wide street slopes down to the water's edge with terraced red brick houses on both flanks, that were formerly occupied by craftsmen who built some of Nelson's fleet from New Forest oak. Great stacks of seasoned timber stood in the village street in those days, when this serene-looking place was a hive of activity central to the nation's defence against Napoleon.

Defence against 'resurrection men' (as grave-robbers were called) accounts for the shelter in the churchyard at **Warblington**, on the mainland opposite Hayling Island. Here village watchmen had to sit through the night to guard against exhumation of their dead by those who profited by supplying specimens to schools of anatomy. Several villages in England still bear signs of their diligence in preventing such macabre practices, but they are more common in the north than in southern England.

Across the Solent, several villages on the Isle of Wight nestle quietly in countryside away from the popular seaside resorts. Dickens wrote part of *David Copperfield* at **Bonchurch**, and the poet Swinburne is buried here, at the Victorian church of St Boniface. The Down above the village is the highest part of the island.

Minstead, Hampshire. The sign of the 'Trusty Servant' inn at this peaceful and unspoilt village is an allegory of the qualities required in the perfect servant.

Bucklers Hard, Hampshire. Shipwrights originally occupied these brick houses beside the wide street where seasoned timber was stacked ready for use in the dockyard.

Godshill, Isle of Wight. This much-photographed village of stone and thatch is one of the island's chief tourist magnets. The church has a painting by Rubens or one of his followers.

Godshill's fame has been much helped by a writer who is happily still with us – J.B. Priestley, O.M. He lived for many years at Brook House, situated high up overlooking the sea at the front and a quarter of the island landscape at the back, and wrote his second volume of autobiography at a time when the steady rain upon Godshill seemed to symbolise the gloom of the approaching war. Godshill's thatched cottages, with the village church behind them, have since become one of the most photographed corners of Britain.

Bembridge is a sedate seaside village with good sands and safe bathing, popular as a sailing centre, but so far unspoiled by commercialism, whilst **Calbourne**, inland, is well known for its pretty row of tiny thatched cottages beside the stream in Winkle Street.

Carisbrooke, near Newport at the centre of the Isle, was once the island capital before Newport overtook it, and the village still has the island's finest church, with its Norman nave and noble Perpendicular tower. But most visitors to Carisbrooke come to see the great stone castle, which stands high above the village, a once-mighty fortress now in ruins, first built by the Normans and hurriedly extended under Queen Elizabeth as part of the national defence against the Armada of Philip of Spain. It was at Carisbrooke that Charles I arrived to take refuge but remained as a prisoner.

Another ruined royal castle is on the mainland at **Corfe**, in Dorset, but it is the village itself which introduces us to that dramatic geological change mentioned at the beginning of this chapter, for we are now on the so-called Isle of Purbeck, where the quarrying of limestone for building is a centuries-old industry. Corfe's own cottages are built of the local grey limestone, and members of the Ancient Order of Marblers and Stonecutters still meet annually in the Town Hall – although ironically this is built partly of brick. Nevertheless, a greater

Winkle Street, Calbourne. This pretty row of cottages is another popular attraction on the Isle of Wight, and the village church is one of the island's oldest.

Corfe Castle, Dorset. The village called by the same name grew up in the shadow of the mighty fortress built to guard a gap in the Purbeck Hills, and blown up after the Civil War.

consistency in village building materials is apparent here for the first time, for we are near the great belt of Jurassic limestone which begins at Portland and sweeps up through the country to the North Yorkshire coast. One of the best places to savour its effect on the style of local villages is at **Abbotsbury**, along the coast. Instead of the mixtures of brick and flint, timber and tile-hanging customary up to this point, Abbotsbury is a village of glowing golden limestone cottages roofed in thatch or slate. The swannery founded by Benedictine monks is its most famous asset, but the consistency of its stone building is a more significant part of the story of village England for anyone arriving from the east.

Villages of stone can be explored up the western side of Dorset with never a brick in sight, and **Burton Bradstock**, **Chideock**, **Stoke Abbott**, **Yetminster**, **Bradford Abbas** and **Trent** are among the best of them. One might expect a village with so delightful a name as **Ryme Intrinseca** to share these glories, but it has been rather spoiled by

modern intrusion, and I mention it only to recall the characteristically lyrical names of many other Dorset villages in the eastern half where stone building is not the universal rule: **Winterbourne Zelstone**, **Fifehead Magdalen**, **Sydling St Nicholas** and **Cerne Abbas** are among them.

Cerne Abbas is better known, like Wilmington in Sussex, for the chalk carving on the hillside above it than for the village itself. The Cerne Giant, flaunting his sexual virility and brandishing a knobbled club, is fondly supposed to date from prehistoric times, having survived the moral outrage of both Benedictine monks and Puritan zealots. I remain sceptical of the figure's antiquity, but applaud Dorset's refusal to have it defaced, even by Victorian moralists. But then, Dorset – arguably England's most unspoilt county – has many undertones of rustic paganism about it, which influenced Thomas Hardy, who lived among the villages of the River Piddle. The river refuses to give up its ancient name and be called Trent instead, and has saddled

Abbotsbury, Dorset. Benedictine monks founded the famous swannery in the fourteenth century, to supply birds for the abbot's table – a taste we have since lost.

Tolpuddle, Dorset. The village green where the famous Tolpuddle Martyrs held their historic meeting in 1831 to protest against their low wages as farmworkers.

villages along its course with names that the more sensitive are embarrassed to pronounce, like **Piddletrenthide** and **Piddlehinton**.

One of them, **Tolpuddle**, seems to have bowed to moralising influences with its slight change of spelling, but this attractive village is not noted for toeing an authoritative line. Here in 1831 six farm labourers met under a sycamore tree at the village centre and raised a joint protest against a reduction of their already pitiful wages. They were promptly arrested and soon sentenced to transportation, but the public's sense of injustice prevailed and the men, already in Australia by that time, were granted a free pardon. They had helped to establish trade union rights, and they became known as the Tolpuddle Martyrs. The sycamore tree is still there, as well as a row of cottages erected as a memorial to the men by the Trades Union Council.

Not to be missed by anyone looking for English villages in all their variety is **Milton Abbas**. It is a curious place, of a kind we shall see more of, set down upon the spot by a landlord who had swept away the original settlement here for the sake of his aesthetic sensibilities: the Earl of Dorchester did not want to see working-class hovels from the windows of his new house. The new village of identical thatched semi-detached cottages all looks very neat and tidy, but it was just the crumb of conscience which the English aristocracy of the time customarily threw to the plebeian masses to save them (the aristocrats) from the fate that befell their counterparts in France. The cruel demolition of whole villages was perpetrated by landlords who did not really care that their occupants were made homeless and reduced to crime and beggary.

Thomas Hardy lived at **Higher Bockhampton**, a thatched hamlet up Cuckoo Lane from the A35 near Dorchester, and the cottage where he wrote

Higher Bockhampton, Dorset. The little-changed cottage where Thomas Hardy was born in 1840, the son of a stone mason. It is now owned by the National Trust.

Far From the Madding Crowd among other work can be visited by appointment. 'It faces west,' as Hardy wrote,

> and round the back and sides
> High beeches, bending, hang a veil of boughs,
> And sweep against the roof . . .

Hardy's grave is in the churchyard at **Stinsford**, but only his heart is buried there, and even that is rumoured to have been eaten by the surgeon's cat. Hardy would have chuckled at this story, but would not have been amused by the insistence of his well-meaning admirers that his body should be interred in Westminster Abbey instead of here among his kinsfolk as he had wished. One of his more recent admirers, C. Day Lewis, is also buried nearby.

In Hardy's fictional peopling of Wessex, he never lost sight of those intimations of the pagan spirit that one still feels in this part of England, and which seems even stronger in Wiltshire, where Salisbury Plain became a kind of focal point for the aspirations of prehistoric settlers of the Stone Age. It is round the fringes of the Plain that we must seek Wiltshire's southern villages, though, and **Avebury**, in a little river valley on the Marlborough Downs, practically sits in the middle of a huge circle of standing stones enclosing 28 acres (11.4 ha) of ground. Those colossal stones, some weighing 40 tons (40.4 tonnes) or more, were set up by men of the Bronze Age

Teffont Evias, Wiltshire. A corner of this pretty village in the valley of the River Nadder, in which each house has its own little stone bridge across the stream.

Fonthill Abbey, Wiltshire. An engraving of the now-destroyed mock-Tudor fantasy built near Fonthill Gifford by the architect James Wyatt for William Beckford.

before the more sophisticated building of Stonehenge was undertaken. No one knows their purpose, but they must have had some profound significance to justify the enormous effort that went into erecting them.

John Aubrey, the antiquary, was the first person to describe the Avebury circle and bring it wider attention. He was born at **Easton Piercy**, near Chippenham, where as a lonely and frail child, he no doubt listened a lot to the village women chattering and picked up his lifelong habit of retailing gossip. Christopher Wren, the great architect, was born six years after Aubrey at **East Knoyle**, where his father was rector.

Megalomania seems to have been the inspiration for the more recent architectural extravaganza which made **Fonthill Gifford** famous. William Beckford inherited the manor from his father and spent a vast fortune in getting James Wyatt to rebuild the family mansion as a neo-Gothic folly

which he called Fonthill Abbey. It was to look like a medieval ruin but include one complete part where he could live. But soon after Beckford – who entertained Nelson and Lady Hamilton here – had sold his hair-raising fantasy to another eccentric, the huge central tower fell down, and little now remains of the place except the high surrounding wall which Beckford built to keep out unwelcome visitors.

Chilmark also supplied stone for rather less ambitious building projects, and its pale creamy white limestone, weathering to a greeny tint, can be seen in the surrounding villages of the Nadder valley. This stone was mined rather than quarried, local workmen bringing it from under the ground as long ago as the thirteenth century for the building of Salisbury Cathedral.

Though Wiltshire has plenty of sheep, it is better known for pigs, and one of the regional specialities here is the 'lardy cake', a spicy currant cake made with the rendered-down fat of the local pigs.

Teffont Evias is a pretty village with houses reached by little stone bridges across a stream, whilst **Wylye** and **Tisbury** display a curious local building practice in their cottages of chequered stone and flint walls. Tisbury is quite large compared with the more characteristic tiny farming villages and hamlets of Wiltshire represented by pairs such as **Codford St Mary** and **Codford St Peter**, or **Ogbourne St George** and **Ogbourne St Andrew**, where some half-timbered houses have brick nogging in the spaces once filled with wattle-and-daub.

Aldbourne, on the Marlborough Downs, is undoubtedly one of the county's most attractive villages, but Wiltshire boasts at least two places which have been called, from time to time, the most beautiful village in England: **Lacock** and **Castle Combe**. Such claims are absurd, since England's villages are all so different they are incomparable, and even Lacock and Castle Combe, though not many miles apart, have such differences that it is impossible to say which one is superior to the other. Lacock belongs to the National Trust, and its streets are lined with houses in a variety of styles and from all periods, one of the oldest being the fourteenth century barn which belonged to the former abbey. Lacock Abbey is the key to the village's fame. It was the last religious house to be dissolved in England,

Chequered flint and stone. A building style popular in parts of Wiltshire, seen here in the walls of a cottage at Wylye, where locally available flint and chalk were used.

and in the seventeenth century it came into the possession of the Talbot family, one of whose members was William Henry Fox Talbot, the pioneer of photography, who carried out his experiments in the mansion built from the abbey ruins. He won the Royal Society Medal for making the first photographic prints, and a museum here houses some of his work.

Lacock Abbey, Wiltshire. The Talbot lords of the manor built this village mansion from the ruins of a nunnery already partly converted to domestic use.

Castle Combe, Wiltshire. Among the most photogenic of English villages, it nestles in a combe formed by the By Brook and welcomes visitors from all over the world.

Castle Combe has the advantage of consistency in its building materials, and this stone village is certainly one of the *prima donnas* of village England, endlessly inviting tourists' snapshots and looking for all the world as if it had been built for that very purpose by someone who realised the commercial potential of Fox Talbot's invention. But Castle Combe has a long history. Wool gave it its importance in medieval times, and the village church reflects its early prosperity. The famous three-arched bridge, which must feature in photograph albums everywhere from Adelaide to Zurich, crosses the little By Brook, which trickles past the Weaver's House where villagers delivered cloth they had woven in their cottages.

The price of modern fame as a showplace is a motorway which misses the village by a hair's breadth and jettisons visitors from far and wide into its little streets – where double yellow lines, car parks and gift shops impair its former rural serenity. But for all that, Castle Combe remains a place of charm and interest, best seen in winter, when it sits quietly and relatively undisturbed in the little combe where Walter de Dunstanville built a castle in the thirteenth century and thus gave the settlement its name.

Altarnun, Cornwall. The church of St Nonna has long been called the 'Cathedral of the Moor'. The village lies at the north-eastern side of Bodmin Moor.

THE WEST COUNTRY

As we travel west the rock gets progressively older and harder, and in Cornwall and parts of Devon we encounter the granite that forms the Atlantic-battered cliffs of Land's End, and which has been used for building in these parts for a surprisingly long time, considering its hardness and resistance to cutting and shaping – you cannot carve fancy ornament from this unyielding rock. The first settlers in these 'tin islands', before the Romans came, built a village of moorland granite at **Chysauster**, near Penzance, close to tin deposits which they worked at least 100 years before the birth of Christ. It is perhaps the oldest village in England, and its remains are still visible with walls standing six feet (1.8 m) high.

Modern and more economical building materials have taken over from the granite nowadays, but there are still villages where the old granite houses and churches stand solid and undefiled (though sometimes whitewashed cement rendering has provided the stone with a coat for its old age). The West Country is an area of startling contrasts. The local

Chysauster, Cornwall. This ancient village of granite houses on the moors near Penzance was built by tin miners before Christ was born, and is among the oldest English villages.

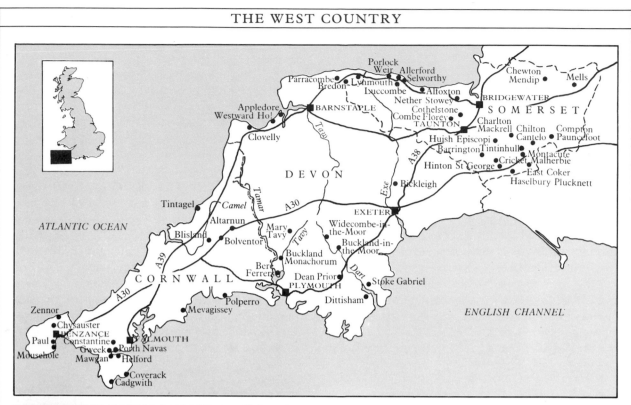

Bench end in Zennor church. The unalluring mermaid carved here represents the more enticing creature who is said to have led the squire's son into the sea.

churches are simple rugged structures totally unlike those in Somerset and Dorset, where the softer limestone lent itself to sumptuous ornament.

Zennor is a characteristic moorland village of plain architecture, more typical of Cornwall's Penwith peninsula than the quaint coastal villages that everyone knows from calendars and chocolate boxes. Tin-mining was the area's *raison d'etre* and the village pub is called the 'Tinners' Arms'. D.H. Lawrence wrote *Women in Love* during a stay here in the First World War – the locals thought Lawrence and his German-born wife Frieda were enemy agents – and the hard-working and hard-living Zennor men must have reminded him of the Nottinghamshire men. The Zennor miners produced music from the bowels of the earth and were as famous for their fine voices as the men in Wales. A bench-end in the church has a carving of a mermaid who is said to have enticed the squire's son to a watery grave when she heard his fine singing.

Most people think of Cornwall in terms of its quaint fishing villages, however, and places like **Mevagissey**, **Polperro**, **Coverack**, **Cadgwith** and **Mousehole** draw millions to tiny villages with steep and narrow streets where small populations of fishermen and their families originally carried on their lives in dread only of the cruel sea – a danger that now seems far less of a threat to life and limb than the traffic converging on these irresistible magnets. Most of these villages have now perforce adopted frontier posts, through which visitors are admitted only after they have deposited their vehicles in large car parks.

Mousehole can hardly blame people for mispronouncing its name – if it wants to be called 'Mouzel' it should change the spelling. Its browny-grey granite cottages tumble down a steep hill to a harbour which was once a centre of pilchard fishing. Most fishing villages in this area were originally just convenient appendages for the fisherfolk of towns set farther back from the sea, and that is why you do not generally find churches in them, though there are often enough Methodist chapels in this region of Wesleyan mass-conversion. **Paul**, half a mile in-land, is Mousehole's 'church town', and in the churchyard is the grave of Dolly Pentreath, wrongly said to be the last person to speak the ancient Cornish tongue. She spoke English well enough, too, as anyone found out who refused to pay sixpence to hear her native language, for then she resorted to abuse that every stranger could understand.

A Cornish woman of more temperate and enticing language has helped to make famous several villages tucked away from the coasts along creeks and inlets, for Daphne du Maurier's stories have used the local landscape to good effect. Villages around the estuary of the Helford River also feature, such as **Porth Navas**, hidden away in a heavily wooded inlet, and **Constantine**, which stands higher up, its houses of slate and granite overlooking the river.

Morwenstow, Cornwall. The village church shows the unornamented style of building in granite forced upon the medieval masons by the unyielding hardness of the material.

Delabole quarry, Cornwall. This vast chasm – one of the largest man-made holes in Britain – is the result of centuries of quarrying the local slate.

Helford, on the south bank of the river, is another idyllic village in a wooded combe, with the 'Shipwright's Arms' as evidence of its one-time preoccupation. Do not confuse it with Helston,

Houses in the village of Delabole with walls and roofs of locally quarried slate. Many souvenirs for the tourists are made from it.

however, the market town farther west where the famous Furry Dance takes place in May. Between the two, on either side of the river, are **Gweek** and **Mawgan,** both quiet little places now, but not always so. Gweek was a busy tin port in medieval times, while Mawgan's former prosperity is evident in its church, with three-storey granite tower and monuments to local families that include a brass to Hannibal Basset, which repeats the same words in four direct lines:

> Shall wee all dye
> wee shall dye all
> all dye shall wee
> dye all wee shall.

Slate is the other native building material of Cornwall, and its main extraction nowadays is at **Delabole,** where one of the largest man-made holes in Britain testifies to the importance of the local quarrying industry over many centuries. The distance round its perimeter is a mile and a half (2.4 km), and you can gaze at it from a viewing platform as if it were the Grand Canyon. The pub here is the 'Bettle and Chisel', named after the quarrymen's tools, and the village houses have both walls and roofs of slate.

Tintagel is also built largely of slate. Its old post office – formerly a manor house – is a well-known vernacular building that has been little changed over the centuries. The National Trust preserves it as the Victorian village post office it subsequently became. The village itself is not among Cornwall's beauties, but then, there is only one thing visitors come here for, and that is King Arthur. The legendary birthplace is well outside the village beneath the cliffs, and nothing can be traced there earlier than a Norman castle, except for a monastery – but this little snag does not deter anyone from clambering down to the rocky promontory in imaginative search for Arthur and Merlin.

Bodmin Moor rises inland to re-assert the predominance of granite, and the hamlet of **Bolventor**, in the middle of this boggy region, boasts Daphne du Maurier's 'Jamaica Inn', which was originally the Bolventor Temperance Hotel before the novelist invested it with the intoxicated romance of her popular tale.

Altarnun and **Blisland** are moorland villages of much character. Altarnun is a quarrying centre, but it is very well kept. As the focus of a very extensive parish, its church is known as the 'Cathedral of the Moor', but Blisland's church of St Proteus and St Hyacinth has been called by John Betjeman 'the most beautiful of all the country churches of the West'. Built of local slate and granite on the village green, it provides an unusual feature of the village where a noted sheep fair is held every September.

As we cross the Tamar into Devon, we temporarily lose sight of the granite, but only until we reach Dartmoor, where the ancient rock again asserts itself in a kind of high island surrounded by the sandstone which forms the county's famous red dairy-farming soil and helps to produce the delicious clotted cream on offer in virtually every village on this lush green county's tourist routes.

Tintagel, Cornwall. The old Post Office here is also built of slate rubble. Originally a small manor house built in the fifteenth century, it is now in the care of the National Trust.

Granite is used for building on Dartmoor itself, but all around it are village houses built of 'cob' – a mixture of mud and straw, pebbles and dung, generally rendered and whitewashed nowadays beneath roofs of thatch – always recognisable by their thick walls and rounded corners. **Buckland-in-the-Moor** is a good place to see granite cottages and **Clovelly** is the best village for cob.

Widecombe-in-the-Moor, a little larger than its neighbour Buckland, is better known for its annual September fair than for its buildings. English-speaking people from all over the world who have never been within a thousand miles of Widecombe are familiar with Old Uncle Tom Cobleigh and all – to say nothing of Tom Pearce's grey mare, which is still said to haunt Dartmoor.

At the edge of Dartmoor on its eastern side is a small place called **Dean Prior**, which sounds holy enough, but Robert Herrick, who was vicar there for a good many years, didn't like Devon much (though he stayed until he died at 83) and gave himself some comfort by writing distinctly unholy love poems:

> Give me a kiss, add to that kiss a score;
> Then to that twenty, add a hundred more:
> A thousand to that hundred: so kiss on,

Clovelly, Devon. The startling gradient of this picturesque coastal village's cobbled main street has kept it naturally traffic-free. At the bottom is a tiny fishing harbour.

Buckland-in-the-Moor, Devon. A secluded village of granite cottages with thatched roofs, it is one of Dartmoor's most charming spots, surrounded by thickly wooded slopes.

To make that thousand up a million.
Treble that million, and when that is done,
Let's kiss afresh, as when we first begun.

Stoke Gabriel and **Dittisham** (where there is a car ferry across the river) are two attractive villages on opposite banks of the River Dart which flows down from the moor to water Totnes and many smaller settlements on its way to the sea.

Allerford, Somerset. The ancient packhorse bridge across the stream stands beside an even older ford which gave the village its name. Smugglers were once active here.

Bickleigh is a stylish little village nestling beside the River Exe beneath the sloping wood. It has a Norman castle with a fine gatehouse, but make sure you find the right village, for there is another Bickleigh in Devon, near Plymouth. This one lies on the A396 between Tiverton and Exeter.

Another riverside village is **Bere Ferrers**. It is relatively inaccessible, for you have to go several miles northward to find a river crossing, but it is a quiet place with a road which ends abruptly beside the lapping waters of the River Tavy.

Cothelstone, Somerset. The gateway to the manor house. Two of Monmouth's rebels were hanged here by Judge Jeffreys in response to criticism of his cruelty by the lord of the manor.

Buckland Monachorum is a pleasant village near the Tamar with Buckland Abbey nearby. After its conversion into a private house following the dissolution of the monasteries, it became the home of Sir Richard Grenville and then Sir Francis Drake, and so is a sort of shrine to English naval heroes, though Drake was a pirate by the reckoning of other maritime nations whose ships he plundered.

A scattered village with the name **Mary Tavy**, nearby, is surrounded by derelict tin and copper mines from which lead, iron and arsenic were often extracted as well. One of the biggest local mines was Wheal Betsy, and the National Trust preserves its engine house north of the village, whose name comes from the church's dedication to St Mary, and the name of the river by which it stands.

Along Devon's Atlantic coastline from the cobbled and traffic-free Clovelly are **Westward Ho!** and **Appledore**, the first named after Charles Kingsley's novel and thus not known before 1855. Appledore is a picturesque fishing village and shipbuilding centre, with characteristic steep streets leading down to the quay where smugglers joined shipwrights and fishermen in making the place a hive of activity, lawful or otherwise.

Lynmouth is remembered for more recent events. It was a quiet herring fishing port until its discovery as a resort – Shelley, Southey and Coleridge were among its early admirers – but it remained relatively unknown until 1952, when it hit the headlines after the River Lyn burst its banks and caused disastrous floods which claimed 31 lives and destroyed many houses and bridges. Now the

Bickleigh, Devon. An attractive riverside village, it is the unlikely site of a Norman castle with a huge gatehouse, long held by the powerful local Courtenay family.

village is restored to its former charm, with thickly wooded gorges rising behind it.

If we cross from Devon to Somerset via Exmoor, we shall find a softer and less forbidding landscape than the Dartmoor area, with many small villages tucked into little valleys, usually thatched and whitewashed, like **Bredon**, but occasionally stone-built, like much of **Allerford**, **Parracombe** and **Porlock Weir**. **Luccombe** and **Selworthy** are among the moor's most attractive villages: the first a secluded and peaceful spot with attractive thatched and colour-washed cottages; the second more famous and much photographed, beautifully situated on a wooded hillside, and having one of those splendid churches which are among the chief features of Somerset's villages. Much of this area is in the protection of the National Trust.

The red sandstone villages round the fringes of the Quantock Hills are well known for their literary associations. The National Trust owns the cottage at **Nether Stowey** where Coleridge lived, and where he wrote *The Ancient Mariner* and *Kubla Khan*. William and Dorothy Wordsworth lived at **Alfoxton** for a while in order to be near their friend, and Dorothy recorded in her journal for February 1898:

Coleridge came in the morning to dinner. Wm and I walked after dinner to Woodlands; the moon and two planets; sharp and frosty. Met a razor-grinder with a soldier's jacket on, a knapsack on his back and a boy to drag his wheel. The sea very black, and making a loud noise as we came through the wood, loud as if disturbed, and the wind was silent.

But the Wordsworths, like the Lawrences a century after them, aroused the suspicion of the natives. Their nocturnal walks and Cumberland accents aroused speculation that they were spying for the French.

Dorothy Wordsworth's acute observation of nature found no echo in the rector of **Combe Florey**, Rev. Sydney Smith, who regarded the country as 'a kind of healthy grave'. He once remarked sarcastically that he 'saw a crow yesterday, and had a distant view of a rabbit today'. But he was nothing if not a merry soul, and his wit carried him through a life which gave pain to no one except perhaps occasionally pompous bishops and politicians. The same could hardly be said of Evelyn Waugh, whose wit was more caustic. He lived in the manor house of this delightful sandstone village for the last ten years of his life.

Cothelstone is an attractive and compact village of red sandstone standing aloof from the main road, but as pretty as a picture on closer acquaintance, with a Jacobean manor house sporting gables and mullioned windows.

Selworthy, Exmoor. Beatrix Potter, among others, thought it a 'perfect village', and the National Trust now owns it. Beyond is Dunkery Beacon, the highest point in Somerset.

Lynmouth, Devon. One of the most popular villages of Devon's Atlantic coastline,

it was formerly a herring fishing port, where Shelley found 'the spirit of beauty'.

The church of St Mary, Huish Episcopi. The tower, built of golden Ham stone, is generally held to be among the finest in a county noted for its splendid churches.

Moving south-eastwards from the hills and moorland of north Somerset, across the Vale of Taunton with its apple orchards growing fruit with unfamiliar names like Bloody Butcher and Slack-ma-Girdle for the local cider mills, we are back in the limestone belt last encountered in Dorset. It is here that we find those gorgeously designed and decorated church towers for which Somerset is famous, and which seem to match the irresistible village names that go with them, such as **Cricket Malherbie** and **Hazelbury Plucknett**. **Huish Episcopi** is one of the best, with a breathtaking fifteenth-century tower 100 feet (30.4 m) high and rich in tiers of pinnacles.

Around Yeovil are several extremely stylish villages built of the mellowed golden limestone from the old quarries on Hamdon Hill, near Montacute. **Hinton St George** has a fine church, well populated with the dead of the Poulett family who were lords of the manor here for many centuries. Not surprisingly, the village inn is called the 'Poulett Arms.'

Montacute is a village of great stylishness at its centre, possessing one of the finest stately homes in

Montacute House, Somerset, viewed from the farm. The house and village are built almost entirely from locally quarried Ham stone.

East Coker, Somerset. Near the church and manor house is this fine row of almshouses, founded around 1640 in the village where T.S.Eliot came to rest in the land of his forbears.

this region, Montacute House, a glowing golden mansion of Elizabethan date built for the Phelips family. Their monuments are in the village church, and they owned the house until it was purchased by the National Trust in 1931. **Tintinhull** and **Barrington** are both quiet villages with fine manor houses also owned by the Trust. Tintinhull is marred, to my mind, only by the preservation of the village stocks, which seem anything but quaint.

East Coker is one of the loveliest villages in Somerset. It was the home of T.S.Eliot's ancestors, who left there in the middle of the seventeenth century to sail to America, and Andrew Eliot (who had been a cordwainer in East Coker where sailcloth used to be made) became the Town Clerk of Boston, Massachusetts. Young Tom Eliot came to England to study at Oxford in 1914 and stayed for the rest of his life. His ashes are buried in the church of this village 'whence his forbears sprang' and which he made the subject of one of his *Four Quartets*.

Compton Pauncefoot, Charlton Mackrell, Chewton Mendip and **Chilton Cantelo** continue Somerset's wealth of delightful and intriguing vil-

lage names farther north, but one of the prize villages at this end of the county answers to the short and sweet name of **Mells**. It has one of the finest churches in this county of fine churches, many charming cottages and farmhouses, and a Tudor manor house which was acquired by one John Horner from Glastonbury Abbey after the Dissolution. He was the abbot's bailiff, and reputedly gained the property by subterfuge – hence little Jack Horner from the nursery rhyme, who 'put in his thumb and pulled out a plum'. The village is graced by several greens and many trees, and the stone here is much greyer than its honey-coloured counterpart in the south of the county. Mells was known to the sons of a Bishop of Manchester, one of whom became a Catholic priest and the other an editor of *Punch*: Father Ronald Knox spent his last years here at Mells Park House, the home of Lord and Lady Oxford; while his brother E.V.Knox had something to say about villages in general very pertinent to this book: 'I cannot choose a favourite, because directly I remember the one that I admired the most I remember another that I admired still more.'

Kilpeck, Hereford & Worcester. This little village has one of the greatest treasures of all English village churches – an unspoiled building brimming with Romanesque carving.

THE HEART OF ENGLAND

VISITORS to the Cotswolds tend to make for the northern end, where the Jurassic rock everyone knows as 'Cotswold stone' is warmer and sunnier than its grey counterpart farther south. In doing so, however, they miss some of the best Cotswold country. The Cotswolds rise in Avon north of Bath and continue 60 miles (96.5 km) north-eastward through Gloucestershire and Oxfordshire, petering out just into Hereford & Worcester and Warwickshire. There is no other part of England where all the buildings – houses, churches, bridges, barns and field walls – are built so consistently of locally quarried stone, and this is what gives the Cotswold villages their happy distinction.

The tiny villages of **Slad** and **Paradise** are characteristic, as is the slightly larger **Sheepscombe** nearby. Stone cottages huddle together on the hillsides as if against the winter cold. Their occupants were busy once in the cloth industry, weaving the coarse wool of the local sheep which made many men rich before predominance in woollen manufacturing passed to Yorkshire. The fine churches of Cotswold villages are often said to have been built 'on the backs of sheep'. The Cotswold villages do not differ from those of Essex or Lincolnshire simply because here it is hilly and there it is flat, nor even because there is abundant stone for building here. What counts most is that the soil provided fine lush pasture for sheep and the limestone gave the area pure streams for fulling wool, so that the area prospered and men built substantial houses and ambitious churches with nature's greatest gift, the stone which local masons had learned to love.

St Briavels, Gloucestershire. The local youth hostel is a medieval castle's thirteenth-century gatehouse, beneath which is a dungeon once used as the local prison.

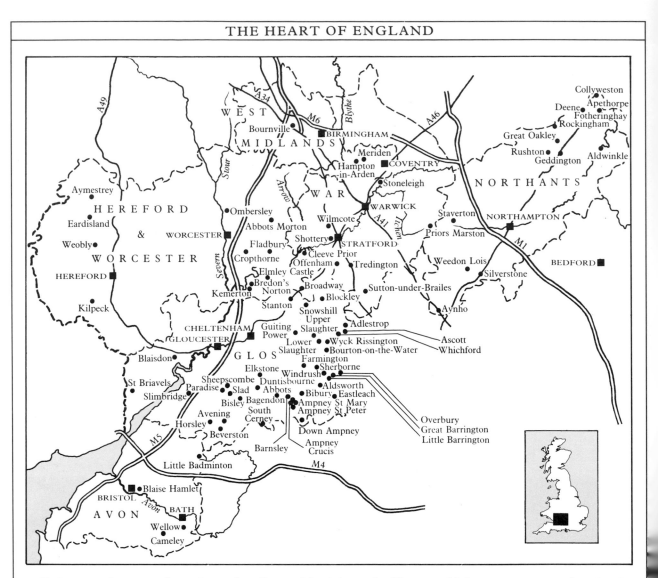

Before getting too deep into the Cotswolds, however, one or two villages should be noted in Avon and in those parts of Gloucestershire bordering both banks of the Severn – the Forest of Dean on the west side and the Vale of Berkeley on the east. **St Briavels** and **Blaisdon** are among the best villages of the forest side, where the settlements are so often spoilt by mining activity. St Briavels has a medieval castle that serves as a spectacular youth hostel, and Blaisdon is well known for its fine plums. On the east side of the estuary, **Slimbridge** needs no introduction as the home of Sir Peter Scott's Wildfowl Trust, where the world's largest collection of wildfowl gathers in the biggest flap of the year.

Among Avon's villages, **Blaise Hamlet** near Bristol is a 'must' to visit, as an example of the 'planned' village as opposed to the 'green' and 'street' villages, which grew more or less haphazardly from an ancient settlement. Blaise Hamlet features the 'cottage ornée' – the idealised country cottage so beloved of wealthy and philanthropic landlords in the nineteenth century. The village consists of individually designed and slightly eccentric cottages grouped round a specially created green, and it was the work of John Nash and George Repton. As a total contrast to this modern conceit, **Wellow** and **Cameley** are worth a look – ancient villages where prehistoric settlers left their marks below the slopes of the Mendip Hills.

Meanwhile, back in the Cotswolds, **Bisley**'s exposure to biting winds long ago gave it its nickname of 'Bisley-God-help-us', but it is an attractive place, with the larger houses built of finely dressed stone, or 'ashlar', and the humbler places of rubble, all watched over by the village church with its broad spire above the main street. There are seven springs in the village which are 'dressed' on Ascension Day in a ceremony more usually associated with Derbyshire.

Avening and Horsley, Little Badminton and Beverston are among the attractive grey villages of the southern Cotswolds, supplemented with Bagendon, Elkstone and Duntisbourne Abbots, built deep in the folds of the hills. Elkstone is the highest of Cotswold villages, and its church sports carvings of grotesque figures and animals.

The Ampneys are an interesting group of four villages consisting of Ampney Crucis, Ampney St Peter, Ampney St Mary, and a stand-offish sister called Down Ampney, which has the distinction of giving birth to the great English composer Ralph Vaughan Williams, to whom there is a memorial in the church.

Among the best known of the central Cotswold villages is Bibury, always densely packed with visitors in summer, but even more attractive at quieter times of the year, when the picture postcard cottages of Arlington Row seem like the rural almshouses they actually are, instead of a group of film stars holding a press conference. The row is separated from the village's main street by the sparkling trout stream, the River Coln, which is crossed by a couple of stone bridges, and opposite is the former mill, now a museum.

Aldsworth, near by, is less known, and is perhaps happy to be so, as it lies sleepily in the valley of the Leach with plenty of space and nothing do disturb its peace except the roaring monsters carved in stone on the string course round the church. Images such as these on the churches of village England must have exerted a powerful influence on illiterate villagers centuries ago. If the graveyards are the books of village history, the gargoyles and grotesques on the church walls must be the books of philosophy, reminding men of the wages of sin.

Bibury, Gloucestershire. One of the best known of Cotswold villages, its bridges cross the River Coln to reach the picturesque almshouse cottages of Arlington Row.

Little Barrington. Matching outfits of mellow stone walls and roofs of stone tiles characterise the Cotswold villages. Many had their own quarries once, and the Strong family owned Barrington's.

Upper Slaughter. One of the most secluded and tranquil villages of the Gloucestershire Cotswolds, its cottages nestle among meadows and bullrushes along the River Eye.

The **Barringtons**, Great and Little, are at the Gloucestershire border in quarrying country where the stone changes from cold grey to buff, and near them are **Windrush, Farmington** and **Sherborne**, each having its own personality. The white stone from Windrush was mined, not quarried, and donkeys were used like pit-ponies in the old days to haul the stone along sloping tunnels to the surface, where it was transported to a wharf at Little Barrington and thence to its waiting customers by river barge. One mine shaft ran beneath the New Inn at Little Barrington's crossroads, and the innkeeper's wife used to stamp on the floor to let the quarrymen know it was time for dinner. Building stone is still quarried at Farmington.

Beyond these villages are the coach-tour Cotswolds, with **Bourton-on-the-Water**, the **Slaughters** and **Broadway** heavily overcrowded and their undoubted charms hidden by a tragic burden of traffic. Other villages are a little quieter and just as beautiful; **Snowshill** on an exposed hillside with its church on a central green; **Stanton**, a street village with mellow stone houses from one end to the other; **Guiting Power**, where the

Cotswold wallers. Dressing stone and constructing a typically neat 'dry' wall of Cotswold limestone in the region where stone remains king of building materials.

Stanton, Gloucestershire. Hard to beat for its appealing mellow stonework, it seemingly soaks up sunshine for letting out like a storage heater in the winter months.

Snowshill Manor. The village's name tells all about its exposed situation in winter. Nevertheless, it is a charming place, with its manor house close to the village green.

Cotswold Farm Park preserves rare breeds of farm animals once close to extinction; **Blockley**, which has a curious history of unlikely industries such as soap-making and pianos.

Broadway, the 'painted lady of the Cotswolds', as it was called somewhat unjustly, takes us across the border into Hereford & Worcester, and it is a convenient point at which to look at other villages of this combined administrative area, where the countryside is full of forestry plantations and orchards, and the traditional drink is locally produced cider. What is distinctive about the villages, however, is the wealth of black-and-white half-timbered buildings.

Weobley, **Aymestrey** and **Ombersley** are typical of the area generally, but **Cropthorne** and **Eardisland**, at opposite ends of the county, are better known for particular corners. Cropthorne's pretty main street running parallel with the Avon has delightful magpie cottages scattered informally along it. **Fladbury**, nearby, is not so pretty in itself, but across a field is the brick-built Fladbury Mill beside the river, which presents as true a picture of unspoilt rural England as one could wish to find anywhere. Eardisland is famous for its much-photographed cottages and gardens beside the little River Arrow.

Eardisland, Hereford & Worcester. The tiny River Arrow flows through this village, pretty as a picture with half-timbered cottages, stone bridges and spring blossom.

Whilst in this western part of the county, no visitor should miss **Kilpeck**. It is worth seeing not so much for the village itself as for the superbly preserved Norman church, which is a priceless treasure of Romanesque carving. The doorway

Cropthorne, Hereford & Worcester. Black and white half-timbered houses are the rule in this eastern area of England where stone is not readily available.

Fladbury Mill. The brick-built mill beside a lock on the River Avon stands not far from the Worcestershire village green with its Anchor Inn and church.

alone is worth making a long journey to see, but the fascinating grotesque figures all round its outside walls make this one of the most riotous architectural sights in Britain as well as a puzzle of medieval symbolism.

The villages of the Vale of Evesham are best seen in springtime, when they wear their new spring costumes of delicately tinted fruit blossom. **Elmley Castle**, **Bredon's Norton** and **Kemerton** are attractive places standing round the foot of Bredon Hill, the site of a more ancient settlement dating back to the Iron Age. **Offenham**, to the east, is one of that small number of English villages which still has a permanent maypole.

Abbots Morton and **Cleeve Prior** are other attractive villages at the eastern extremity of the county, whilst **Overbury** brings us back to the Cotswold fringes, its stone houses mingling with brick and half-timbered ones in a curiously untypical but very refined and well-kept way. The banker family of Martins have been lords of the manor here for 300 years.

Almost every village in the Cotswolds has its own little claim to fame. **Adlestrop** is where a train making an unscheduled stop gave the poet Edward Thomas a glimpse of local birds and plants and inspired a fine poem; **Wyck Rissington** gave Gustav Holst his first job, as organist in the village church, where he was regarded as 'a young man with great promise'; **Eastleach** was latterly the home of Nadia Benois, the artist and theatre designer and mother of Peter Ustinov.

These individual distinctions, however, are nothing compared with the collective stylishness and cosy solidity of villages and countryside which Sydney Smith inexplicably called 'this region of stone and sorrow', and William Cobbett thought the ugliest thing he had seen in his life. Were they both being mischievously provocative? Probably not, for it was only with the coming of the railways and the greater ease of travel that large numbers of townsfolk began to see rural England with a fresh eye and appreciate that the villages were almost a lost heritage as far as the industrialised urban areas of Britain were concerned.

The Cotswolds were a benighted and unsophisticated region before modern industry and communications made England an altogether smaller place. Remote hill villages were given to primitive superstition and folklore, a fact reflected in the many modern plays for stage, television and radio which are set in the area and deal with sinister themes. At **Barnsley**, near the Roman road known as Akeman Street, eight skeletons dug up at an inn called 'Ready Token' were popularly supposed to be the remains of travellers robbed and murdered by the innkeeper. At **South Cerney**, in 1785, the

ecclesiastical court exacted ritual penance from William Stephens for what was called 'the foul sin of fornication' – although he was merely unlucky to be betrayed by a tell-tale, for the Church knew as well as everyone else that the people had little other than 'country matters' to occupy their spare time. Witchcraft throve in isolated villages where the illiterate lived in constant unease at the powers of the unknown.

There are precious few picturesque villages in that new county unhappily named West Midlands, necessitating a careful distinction between the county and what was always a convenient regional title for the area here called 'Heart of England'. There is **Bournville**, of course, the Cadburys' industrial garden village now lending a touch of class to the ever-spreading blot on the map of England which represents Birmingham; and just for curiosity, there is **Meriden**, where the village cross is so often said to be the exact geographical centre of England, though how that statistic is computed is beyond my understanding.

Still, we have not quite finished with the Cotswolds yet (even apart from the Oxfordshire section which follows in another chapter), for as well

The Triangle or Public Gardens at Bournville

BRIEF POINTS ABOUT THE BOURNVILLE VILLAGE TRUST

Average garden space allowed to each house	600 sq. yd.
Estimated return from cultivation of garden plot per week	2s. to 3s.
Width of tree-lined roads	42 ft.
Extent of the Bournville estate	over 400 acres
Rents in Bournville range from (rates not included)	6s. 6d.
A week to (rates included)	9s.
Area of sports ground	12½ acres

DIMENSIONS OF SMALLEST DWELLINGS IN BOURNVILLE VILLAGE

Ground floor—	
Living room or kitchen	16 ft. 6 in. by 11 ft. 6 in.
Parlour	13 ft. 6 in. by 11 ft. and bay window
Scullery	7 ft. by 7 ft. 6 in.
Lobby larder	
First floor—	
Bedroom	13 ft. 6 in. by 11 ft.
Bedroom	11 ft. 6 in. by 9 ft.
Bedroom	7 ft. 3 in. by 8 ft. 9 in.
Linen closet	

A Garden City Cricket Pavilion
The pavilion at Bournville contains a well-equipped gymnasium, refreshment, and dressing-rooms

Houses which can be Made to Pay
They are pleasantly designed, variety of effect being definitely striven for

Bournville, West Midlands. An early twentieth-century prospectus for the Quaker Cadburys' model village begun in 1879. It was not exclusive to chocolate factory workers.

as Broadway, which took us into Hereford & Worcester, there are **Ascott**, **Whichford**, **Tredington** and **Sutton-under-Brailes**, which take us into Warwickshire and where, farther north, leafy lanes link the villages of country familiar to Shakespeare.

Shottery is well enough known, where Anne Hathaway lived in her parents' 'cottage' of a dozen rooms before her beloved William took her off to Stratford, and here there is a big difference from the Cotswold villages we have left behind. Instead of the stone walls and roofs and stone-defined fields, we are now in country where fields with hedges surround villages built of brick and timber, often with roofs of thatch.

Wilmcote is where Shakespeare's mother, Mary Arden, was born in a typical local Tudor farmhouse, and **Charlecote** is where her irrepressible son is said to have poached deer in Sir Thomas Lucy's great park. All these places featuring in Shakespeare's life and legend are open to the public, and **Hampton-in-Arden** is a village which belongs with them in style and character.

Stoneleigh, near Kenilworth, is a small and attractive village where a Cistercian abbey once stood, founded in 1154 and carrying on its quiet religious life for 400 years until the Dissolution. Nothing but the gatehouse now remains intact and except for this one relic, all those centuries of dedication by men acting according to their honest convictions have been totally erased as if they had never happened.

Priors Marston is reached by a long straight lane from Southam called Welsh Road – and what a surprise greets us at the end of it. Here, after all the brick and timber of north Warwickshire, we suddenly find ourselves well and truly back in stone country, with a beautifully kept village of rich brown colour. The limestone here is of a different nature from that in the Cotswolds, being coarser and tinted by iron oxide in the rock, and this serves as a splendid introduction to what is perhaps one of the most underrated counties of England, from the point of view of its villages.

Northamptonshire's northern villages are scattered about the belt of limestone which continues north-eastwards from the Cotswolds and travels right up through the east Midlands and into

Anne Hathaway's 'cottage'. The house at Shottery, Warwickshire, where Shakespeare's wife grew up until she was married – already pregnant – to the young actor. It was then Hewlands Farm.

Priors Marston, Warwickshire. A cosy brown ironstone village once noted for making chairs. It comes as a surprise when approached from the north, where brick and timber predominate.

Yorkshire. What mainly distinguishes these villages from all those we have seen hitherto is their colour. The 'ironstone' of these parts is responsible for the iron and steel industries of the Corby area, but it has also provided building stone which lends a tanned warmth to country villages which sometimes nestle close to places like Kettering, Wellingborough and Corby itself, as if they were sunburnt children clinging to their mothers' skirts. In actual fact, of course, the villages would be more accurately described as the parents of the industrial towns.

Standing almost in the shadows of the foundry chimneys of Corby is **Great Oakley**, an unbelievably peaceful little place, whilst **Geddington** and **Rushton** are hardly a stone's throw away, and **Rockingham** is even closer. Yet this latter street village on a steep hill beside the River Welland has preserved the country character which Dickens knew when Corby itself was only a sleepy village in the fields. For the novelist was an occasional guest of the Weston family at Rockingham Castle, originally built long ago to guard a crossing of the river. It

Rockingham, Northamptonshire. A thatcher works on the roof of a cottage in this attractive street village overlooking the valley of the River Welland.

stands at the top of the village with a curiously unattractive church, presiding, as it were, over the villagers whose cottages stretch down the hill towards the valley below.

The pride of Geddington is the finest of the surviving Eleanor Crosses, those symbols of love and grief which Edward I erected at every resting place of Eleanor of Castile's body on its journey to London for royal burial in Westminster Abbey. 'In life I loved her dearly, nor can I cease to love her in death,' the king wrote, and this restrained medieval monument, built of locally quarried limestone, still stands as witness to the old warrior's sincerity.

Nothing royal remains standing at **Fotheringhay**, a village of even less happy memories, for here at the once-mighty castle where only an earthwork now reveals its site, Richard III was born and Mary Queen of Scots put to death. But the village has an air of dignity about it as if it remembers its former importance, and its church has a rare elegance, with its octagonal lantern and flying buttresses.

Deene, Apethorpe and **Aldwinkle** (where the poet John Dryden was born) are among other attractive villages at this end of Northamptonshire, and **Collyweston** is a place to which thousands of people in the Midlands have long been indebted for providing roofs over their heads. The Romans made use of Collyweston stone tiles, and they are still used today, thin and lightweight slabs of stone mined from the limestone beds which weather to an attractive greeny-brown. Unlike the Welsh slateworkers, the village quarrymen here get the weather to do their splitting. The stone slabs are put out in the open and well watered during frosty weather. As the water which seeps into the stone freezes, it expands and splits the slabs into ideal thicknesses.

Staverton, near Daventry, is another fine stone village with cottages along its winding lanes off the

Aynho, Northamptonshire. Apricot trees grow on the walls of this stylish dove-grey hilltop village, where the houses face the lord of the manor's place, Aynhoe Park.

main road, but farther south, we return to the paler limestone which will lead us conveniently into the Oxfordshire Cotswolds in the next chapter. **Silverstone's** name is evidence enough of what once was, but there is little pale grey stone visible now in this village inseparably associated with motor racing. Nor does **Weedon Lois** retain much stone among its modern brickwork, apart from a fine headstone, designed by Henry Moore, marking the grave of Edith Sitwell in the cemetery.

Undoubtedly the most stylish village in this corner of Northamptonshire is **Aynho**. It stands beside the frantic A41 near the Oxfordshire border, on a hilltop site, and is built so consistently and attractively of dove-grey limestone that it looks like a modern estate village, and indeed it partly is, for the big house, Aynhoe Park, is across the road from the cottages. The village is an old place, nevertheless, and quiet little lanes with names like Skittle Alley are tucked away within touching distance of the trunk road, whilst the house walls often sport apricot trees and the village square has one or two shops as well as thatched cottages. It is said that the apricot trees were first planted to provide fruit to pay tolls to the Cartwright lords of the manor.

The Eleanor Cross at Geddington. At the village centre is one of three surviving monuments put up by Edward I along the route used in taking his wife's body to London.

Swan Upping at Cookham. *One of a large number of paintings by Stanley Spencer of his native Berkshire village, this is also among the least controversial.*

THAMES AND CHILTERNS

OXFORDSHIRE is separated from Northamptonshire near Aynho by a tributary of the Thames, the River Cherwell, and just across the water is **Adderbury**, as different from its near neighbour as chalk from cheese. The pale limestone of Aynho is here replaced by brown ironstone once more, and the large village looks as though it were built of toffee. A brook bisects the village, its two parts each having a green, but the parish church of St Mary in the eastern half is the main attraction here, for its walls display a wealth of weird Norman carvings of human, animal and mythological figures including gryphons, mermaids and dragons.

The mason who carved them also worked at **Bloxham**, where the parish priest was hanged from the church tower in 1544 for opposing the English Litany. Rivalry between the two villages even extends to their church spires, one local expression being 'Bloxham for length, Adderbury for strength', but Adderbury folk, once busy weaving woollen cloth, used to say that 'Bloxham dogs come to Adderbury to buy their togs'. It is a matter of taste whether Adderbury's claim to superiority is enhanced or betrayed by the fact that the Earl of Rochester, that profligate Restoration poet, lived here at Adderbury House. He was already in the Tower before he was twenty, for seducing another man's betrothed, and it was he who wrote the famous epitaph on Charles II, whom he had dubbed the 'merry monarch':

> Here lies our Sovereign Lord the King,
>   Whose word no man relies on,
> Who never said a foolish thing,
>   Nor ever did a wise one.

Great Tew is another of Oxfordshire's tawny ironstone villages well known for its pretty thatched cottages with their little front gardens facing the village green, and here again we see the geological dividing line between the Liassic limestone, which gives us the coarse but colourful ironstone, and the Oolitic, which provides finer-grained building stone of lighter hue, for **Sandford St Martin**, only a few

Fettiplace monument, Swinbrook, Oxfordshire. This extraordinary trio, apparently about to perform a dance routine in a Tudor cabaret, is one of two such family monuments.

67

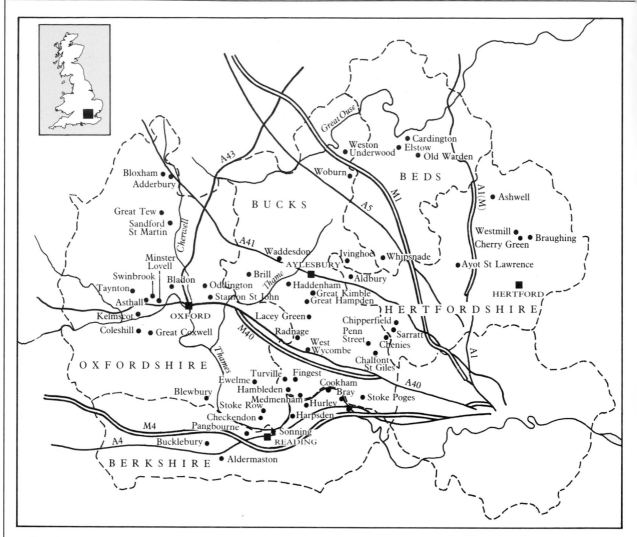

miles along a country road, is distinctly grey.

We are back in the Cotswold country here, and Oxfordshire's Cotswold fringe boasts many attractive villages, not least among them being **Swinbrook**, where old stone cottages are scattered about a peaceful village on the River Windrush, where the Mitford sisters lived in the manor house rebuilt by their father Lord Redesdale. Nancy and Unity are both buried in the churchyard, Nancy's headstone bearing the image of a mole, as she had always been fond of these animals and did not want a cross – a symbol of torture – on her grave. The church itself is filled to overflowing with the tombs of an older local family, the Fettiplace lords of the manor. Their effigies are stacked up – there is no other word for it – in sets of three on shelves against the north wall; half a dozen recumbent old soldiers resting in bunk beds and waiting for reveille.

Asthall is the neighbouring village, and very pretty it is too, but it has a typical Cotswold ghost story to tell. In an old farmhouse which once stood near the village, an old woman practised baby farming. But having taken the money for their maintenance from the parents, she murdered the babies and buried them in the garden, and long afterwards at midnight a lamp could be seen moving about the spot – and still can for all I know – as the old woman's ghost went about her grisly business.

A little further downstream is **Minster Lovell**, where more macabre stories are told of the ruined manor house by the riverside. It was built by the Lovell family, of whom Francis was one of Richard III's closest friends and allies. After the king's death at Bosworth, Lovell joined the rebellion against Henry Tudor and, fleeing from a battle in which the rebels were soundly beaten, he is said to have taken

The church of St Mary, Adderbury. Among the finest of Oxfordshire parish churches, it ably represents the large wealthy village, with fascinating medieval carvings outside.

refuge in a secret vault at Minster Lovell where he was fed by a loyal servant who had the only key. But the secret died with the servant, and Lord Lovell was buried alive. The village's attractive 'Old Swan' inn is a welcome restorative after seeing the site of this gruesome tale.

In the opposite direction on the north side of the river lies **Taynton**, one of England's most important former quarrying villages. The quarries here were mentioned in Domesday Book, and the medieval villagers were accustomed to seeing great cartloads of brown limestone being hauled away by teams of oxen or horses for building places such as Blenheim Palace, Windsor Castle and the Oxford colleges.

Farther south at the edge of Oxfordshire's Cotswolds, **Kelmscot** is well known as the home of William Morris. He lived in the grey manor house for twenty-five years, and the high stone walls round its garden protected the villagers from the animated conversation and questionable morals of Pre-Raphaelite guests such as Dante Gabriel Rossetti and his sister Christina, Edward Burne-Jones, Ford Madox Brown and W. B. Yeats. Rossetti flirted with Morris's wife Jane as he painted her portrait, but tired of the place which he called 'the doziest clump of old grey beehives'. But Morris so loved the place that he gave its name to the private press on which he produced beautiful books such as *News from Nowhere*, in which an illustration of the house formed the frontispiece. He and Jane are buried in the churchyard beneath a long gravestone which is fast decaying.

It was William Morris who likened the huge tithe barn at **Great Coxwell** to a cathedral, and if the village itself is not so pretty as next-door **Coleshill**, which the National Trust owns, the barn alone puts Coxwell on the essential itinerary for this region. Village England may offer no cathedrals, but it boasts no more awe-inspiring building than this

The Maytime Inn, Asthall. A characteristic village of the Oxfordshire Cotswolds, Asthall is a stone-built place with fine

Cottages at Great Tew, Oxfordshire. This village of brown stone and thatch was laid out by the young J.C.Loudon in 1808 for the lord of the manor, General Stratton.

church and manor house in the valley of the Windrush.

great barn, erected in oak and stone by the Cistercian monks of Beaulieu Abbey in the thirteenth century, and perfectly preserved after 700 years.

Nearer Oxford, **Bladon** is well known as the village where the Churchills lie buried. Not for this great family the mighty monuments of marble and alabaster in noble churches – their graves are marked by simple headstones set close together in a typical English churchyard, Sir Winston among them, at home, as it were, with his family about him.

North east of Oxford is a bleak and uninhabited area of drained marshland called Otmoor, and one or two of the villages round its fringes have some interest for the dedicated village enthusiast, though their mixtures of building materials make them something of an anti-climax in visual terms after the delights of Cotswold stonework. Some were the scenes of much social disturbance in the nineteenth century, when forty years of agitation from wealthy landowners, including the Duke of Marlborough, finally won an order for drainage and enclosure of the marsh. Local villagers who had held grazing rights from time immemorial took the law into their own hands to defeat this iniquitous injustice, destroying bridges, smashing down fences and hedges, and driving their cattle on to freshly ploughed fields. Troops were called in to quell the riots, but disturbances continued for five years before the local people resigned themselves to defeat, their complaint immortalized in a neat anonymous verse:

Great Coxwell, Oxfordshire. The magnificent tithe barn of stone and timber belonged to Beaulieu Abbey, and has stood 'as noble as a cathedral', as Morris said, for 700 years.

The fault is great in man or woman
Who steals a goose from off a common.
But what can plead that man's excuse
Who steals a common from a goose?

Oddington's chief claim to fame, apart from its participation in these events, is the gruesome brass in its church to Ralph Hamsterley, a sixteenth-century parson who is represented in a shroud being consumed by worms. **Stanton St John** was the home of John Milton's grandfather and of the modern storyteller A.E. Coppard, who threw up his regular job to become a professional writer. He lived in extreme poverty here until his stories *Adam and Eve and Pinch Me* brought him well deserved recognition.

Oxfordshire is doubly fortunate in having the Cotswolds running through one end of the county and the Chilterns through the other, but before we consider the very different but equally interesting villages of the Chiltern Hills, we should see what the royal county of Berkshire has to offer us. Chunks of it were transferred to Oxfordshire in the recent boundary changes, but what remains is delightful Thames valley country with many fine villages.

If **Aldermaston** is famous for the wrong reasons, that should not deter anyone from seeing this attractive street village of brick houses with a brick-built mill and an inn with a village lock-up behind it.

Blewbury and **Bucklebury** are among other charming villages of west Berkshire, with some half-timbered houses taking their places alongside the old and mellow brickwork. **Hurley** is one of the best Thames-side villages, where punting on the river is a popular way to spend a lazy summer afternoon.

Bray is celebrated for the vicar who switched his religion to suit the prevailing climate of opinion, whilst **Cookham** is known for its native and controversial artist, Stanley Spencer. He peopled his bizarre religious paintings with local folk in local settings, and the Stanley Spencer Gallery, in the old village hall, displays drawings, paintings and personal effects of this famous or notorious son of Cookham, who was wont to trudge through the village with his painting utensils in an old pram. He was buried in the churchyard which had formed the background to so many of his artistic fantasies. Both these villages deserve notice for their riverside beauty, and Cookham has other curiosities such as a handless clock and a notice which officially orders 'all fighting to be over by 10 p.m.'

Sonning continues the Thames-side theme – a secluded village with one of the oldest Thames bridges spanning the river with no less than eleven arches. The Bishops of Salisbury once had a palace in this village where brick and half-timbering join hands beneath roofs of thatch.

Hurley, Berkshire. This is one of the sedate Thames-side villages where a lazy summer afternoon on the river is the recommended way to enjoy them most.

Maharajah's Well, Stoke Row. The Maharajah of Benares made a gift of this well to the village in the Oxfordshire Chilterns when he heard of its water difficulties.

Pangbourne is a larger and busier place upstream. Kenneth Grahame, author of *The Wind in the Willows*, lived here and it featured in Jerome K. Jerome's *Three Men in a Boat*. Pangbourne marks that stretch of the Thames where chalk hills begin to rise on both sides – those stretching southward forming the Berkshire Downs and those north of the river the Chiltern Hills.

The Oxfordshire Chilterns are more heavily wooded than the more northerly parts of this range of chalk uplands, and some say they are the finest part, though clearly that is a matter of taste. Certainly there is much secluded beauty in these beech-clad hills, but one of the keys to their nature is their relative dryness, for no river or stream crosses the range in its whole course through Oxfordshire, Buckinghamshire, Hertfordshire and Bedfordshire, and this singular fact accounts for the sparse population of the hills up to recent times.

At **Stoke Row** is an eccentric-looking symbol of the water shortage. Edward Reade of nearby Ipsden (father of Charles Reade, author of *The Cloister and the Hearth*) was Governor of the North West Provinces in India. He happened to remark to the Maharajah of Benares one day about the difficulty experienced at Stoke Row, near his home in England, in obtaining water, and the Prince undertook to finance the provision of a well, which was dug 368 feet (118.8 m) deep and completed in 1864. And there it stands to this day amid the village's council houses, with a distinctly oriental cupola over it and an elephant above the winding gear.

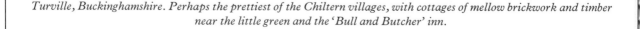

Turville, Buckinghamshire. Perhaps the prettiest of the Chiltern villages, with cottages of mellow brickwork and timber near the little green and the 'Bull and Butcher' inn.

Fingest, Buckinghamshire. The twin saddleback tower of the Norman church is a distinctive feature of one of the best Chiltern villages, tucked well into the hills.

Checkendon, nearby, has one of the best of the smaller Chiltern churches, with a rounded Norman apse, while **Harpsden**, near Henley-on-Thames, features an architectural eccentricity in the form of barn walls made of old wallpaper printing blocks.

The real treasure of the Oxfordshire Chilterns, however, is **Ewelme**, nestling beneath the western escarpment. Jerome K. Jerome is buried in the churchyard of this ancient brick village to which Thomas Montacute, Earl of Salisbury, came with his bride Alice Chaucer, grand-daughter of the poet. She had inherited the manor from her father. They began a rebuilding programme incorporating their palace, a school and a hospital for thirteen poor men, attached to the rebuilt church. After the Duke (for he had been promoted by that time) met his ignominious end in a boat off Calais, the Duchess completed the building here and lived in the palace until her own death, when she was buried in the church beneath a magnificent alabaster monument which is unquestionably one of the great works of art of village England. The mellow brick school and almshouses she built are still in use – the oldest surviving brick buildings in the Chilterns – near the stream which runs through the village's watercress beds.

Continuing through the Chilterns into Buckinghamshire we soon come upon **Turville** and **Fingest**, as pretty a pair as can be found anywhere, secluded along single-track roads in their own little valley between the sloping beechwoods. Turville has an old smock-mill, converted into a dwelling house, that stands over it like a guardian angel with outstretched wings. Its centre is the picture of innocence, but an unsolved murder casts its ancient shadow over this quiet place, for a thirteenth-century stone coffin found beneath the floor of the church contained, not the skeleton of a medieval priest as might have been expected, but that of a woman with a hole in her head.

Fingest is a little more haphazard than neatly-preserved Turville, but it presents an image of English rural life and continuity that is hard to beat, particularly if you climb the hill to Hanger Wood and look down on the village with its Norman church, which has a rare twin saddleback roof.

Hambleden, Buckinghamshire. The weatherboarded and much-photographed mill on the Thames is at the Mill End of this delightful Chilterns village.

HAMBLEDEN, to the south, is a pretty village but best known for its much photographed mill beside the Thames, some distance from the village centre; while **Medmenham**, not far away, was the scene of disreputable eighteenth-century goings-on in a converted abbey. Here, members of the Hell-Fire Club, dubbed the 'Monks of Medmenham' – who included a Chancellor of the Exchequer, a First Lord of the Admiralty, a Paymaster General, a Governor of Bengal and other distinguished men of various positions and assorted morals – met to hold drinking parties and enjoy sexual adventures with the loose women they called their 'nuns.'

Sir Francis Dashwood, the founder and chief priest of this bizarre congregation, lived at **West Wycombe**, a village now owned by the National Trust, and he rebuilt the village church in Byzantine style with a golden globe on top of the tower, in which three could sit and have a drinking party – 'the best Globe tavern I was ever in' as John Wilkes called it. Dashwood also built the extraordinary pagan mausoleum of flint on West Wycombe Hill where his family and some of his friends were interred.

Unorthodox behaviour was a hallmark of the scattered Chiltern inhabitants. Such villages as there were in medieval times housed lawless folk who robbed travellers and were born Nonconformists. **Chalfont St Giles** has the cottage where John Milton spent some time when the plague was

Milton's Cottage, Chalfont St Giles. It was not actually Milton's, but he lived here when the plague drove him out of London, and may have completed Paradise Lost *here.*

West Wycombe, Buckinghamshire. The church originally served a lost medieval village, but was rebuilt by Sir Francis Dashwood with the golden ball in which men could sit.

raging in London, and where he is said to have completed *Paradise Lost*. The cottage belonged to his Quaker friend Thomas Ellwood, who is buried at Jordans, nearby, with more distinguished members of the Society of Friends, including William Penn, the most influential of George Fox's disciples. **Great Hampden** was the home of the famous John Hampden who refused to pay Ship Money to Charles I, and a copy of the document recording this historic defiance is in the church at **Great Kimble**, for it was at a parish meeting here that Hampden took his courageous decision.

The Chiltern villages also housed poor folk who took no part in great issues, but carried on their hard-working lives as chair-bodgers or straw plaiters. The bodgers were woodland craftsmen who made chair legs from the local beeches for the furniture factories in and around High Wycombe. Straw plaiting was a cottage industry in which women worked long hours to supplement the poor incomes of their menfolk.

Some of the quietest and most typical Chiltern country is around isolated hill villages like **Radnage** and **Lacey Green**, where Rupert Brooke spent happy weekends at the 'Pink and Lily' before going off to some foreign field. **Penn Street** brings village cricket back to mind with its delightful inn sign 'The Hit or Miss'. The wisteria-clad brick inn beside the village pitch was once part of a chair factory, where the workers were apt to be called 'chairopodists' like the woodland bodgers.

Chenies, across the other side of the hills, is a model village built by the earls of Bedford, and their former manor house (before they moved to Woburn Abbey), with its ornamental Tudor brick chimneys, can be visited, though their sumptuous monuments in the nearby church can only be glimpsed through the glass of the Bedford Chapel wall. Lord John

Braughing, Hertfordshire. The ford across the River Rib was known to soldiers of the Roman army, and can still be crossed by modern chariots when the village ducks are not standing in it.

Russell, the Prime Minister, lies here among his relations, the earls, dukes, countesses, *et al.*

From here we pass over into Hertfordshire, where **Sarratt** and **Chipperfield** are typical local villages with large greens popular with horse-riders, who are legion in these parts, and where **Aldbury** is an irresistible magnet, with its mellow brick houses round the village duckpond. The Chilterns peter out as they push into Bedfordshire, but not before

Stoke Poges church, Buckinghamshire. This is the church yard in which Thomas Gray is supposed to have written his Elegy, and where he is buried. A monument to him is nearby.

Not all the villages of these northern home counties are in the Chilterns, of course, and on the London side of Buckinghamshire is **Stoke Poges**, where Thomas Gray is buried in the churchyard in which he is said to have written his famous *Elegy*.

On the Aylesbury side of the county, **Haddenham**, **Waddesdon** and **Brill** have their various attractions. Haddenham is a large commuter village, which nevertheless has a highly attractive centre and is a trifle eccentric in containing not only a Station Road without a railway (which is not so uncommon nowadays) but also a High Street which is a *cul-de-sac*. Waddesdon is a much more formal street village on A41, with the Rothschild chateau-style mansion lording it over the village. Brill is a picture of informal village growth, with its windmill on the hilltop overlooking the Oxfordshire plain.

Weston Underwood, in the north of the county, is a stylish street village where William Cowper was installed by his friends the Throckmortons at Weston Lodge, where he had views over the fields from his window-seats and was able to retain some fragile peace of mind and write much good poetry. The village inn is called 'Cowper's Oak' after the tree he used to sit under.

Bedfordshire, the county which makes the bricks for the houses of the stone-free south eastern

Westmill, Hertfordshire. The old pump on the green of this attractive village in one of the more rural corners of an extremely pressurised county was well known to Charles Lamb.

they have embraced **Ivinghoe**, an attractive village below the hill known as the Beacon, and **Whipsnade**, which hardly needs any introduction as the site of the famous zoo: Bactrian camels, among other creatures, now roam in what a seventh-century monk called 'the deserts of Chiltern'.

Ivinghoe has rarer things to see, too, such as its old thatch-hook and the hour-glass affixed to the church pulpit, to tell the more conscientious preacher that his time was up. The thatch-hook was an invaluable tool in the days when most village dwellings were thatched and there was no fire brigade. The long hook was used to pull off burning thatch from the roof and thereby hopefully save the rest of the building from total destruction.

Brill, Buckinghamshire. The ancient weatherboarded post mill occupying the highest point of this hilltop village is a well known landmark and affords fine views.

counties of England, is not specially noted for the prettiness of its villages, but it does have one or two interesting ones. **Elstow**, near Bedford, is where John Bunyan spent his early years, living with his parents not far from the place of his birth. The old brick Moot Hall displays items of his time there, while the village church has memorial windows with scenes from *The Pilgrim's Progress*.

Cardington, now a less-than-beautiful dormitory village where the ill-fated R101 airship was built in the enormous hangars of its nearby airfield, was once the home of John Howard, the great prison reformer, whose house can still be seen near the church. The church itself contains fine monuments to members of the Whitbread brewing family, who were lords of the manor.

Manorial landlords built **Old Warden** and **Woburn** as estate villages. The former is famous for the Shuttleworth Collection of old aircraft and vintage cars at the nearby airfield; and the latter is best known for the highly commercialised Woburn Abbey, where the Dukes of Bedford moved after

leaving Chenies. Some of the Woburn cottages were built without front doors, as the Duke could not bear to see women gossiping at their doorways as he passed through.

Hertfordshire boasts several splendid villages besides those in its Chiltern corner, and **Ayot St Lawrence**, **Westmill**, **Braughing** and **Ashwell** are among the most noteworthy, all with the village greens very common in this county. Ayot St Lawrence is so well known as the home of the sage George Bernard Shaw that its other attractions are easily overlooked, but Shaw and his wife chose it as a place convenient for London and yet quiet and secluded, and so it miraculously remains, in this county which is overpopulated to bursting point. Ayot is a leafy place with nice old houses, a ruined church, and a modern Grecian-style church across a field, which created much controversy when first built. It was called a 'heathen temple' by those who liked their churches to be more traditional.

Ashwell's church is more conventional, with one of the best examples of the diminutive local steeple known as the 'Hertfordshire spike'. But this ancient settlement near a spring surrounded by ash trees – the source of the River Cam – brings a slight shiver of apprehension to visitors who know its history, for part of Ashwell's story is literally written in its stones. The Black Death struck the village in 1349, and as the villagers brought their dead into the fields, a literate villager – perhaps a monk – scratched a desperate message in Latin on the wall of the church: 'Wretched, wild, distracted, the dregs of the people alone survive to witness.'

Westmill restores a happier note. Besides its own attractions it has the nearby hamlet of **Cherry Green**, where Charles Lamb purchased the only property he ever owned, the diminutive cottage called Button Snap ('Goo aan oop theer', said an old man directing me to it). This lover of Hertfordshire never lived in it, however, a piece of irony like the local humour, which explains the rosemary growing in village gardens thus: 'They do say it only grows where the missis is maaster, and it do grow 'ere loike woild foire.'

St Mary's church, Ashwell. One of the best examples of the short and slender local spire known as the 'Hertfordshire Spike' surmounts a village church full of fascination.

The village sign at Castle Acre, Norfolk, showing the priory. It was carved by Harry Carter in 1951 to commemorate the Festival of Britain.

THE EASTERN COUNTIES

CROSSING from Hertfordshire into Essex can be a misleading introduction to the nature of eastern England, for we have first the vast royal hunting ground of Epping Forest, followed by some busy industrial areas between Chelmsford and the Thames, and a constant heavy flow of traffic. Nevertheless, one local distinction that deserves mention is that **Great Wakering**, a village between Southend and Foulness, is in the Guinness Book of Records as the driest spot in Britain, with an average rainfall of about 19 inches (48.2 cm) a year.

For more characteristic scenes, the area around Colchester offers a more promising start, containing villages such as **Tolleshunt d'Arcy** and **St Osyth**.

D'Arcy is the largest of three Tolleshunt villages, the others being Knights and Major. Tolleshunt d'Arcy has the Tudor manor house of the d'Arcy lords of the manor, whose monuments are in the village church. St Osyth boasts the finely preserved buildings of a priory established here by the Bishop of London in the twelfth century and dedicated to Osyth, the daughter of an Anglian king, who had founded a nunnery here long before. The buildings are enhanced by fine gardens.

Over to the west, between Harlow and Chelmsford, is a cluster of villages called the Rodings, known by locals as the 'Rootings', and here we find the farming country more typical of East Anglia,

St Osyth's Priory, Essex. The well-preserved priory buildings are enhanced by fine formal gardens created in the eighteenth century for Lord Rochford.

THE WASH

Cley-next-the-Sea
● Burnham Thorpe
● Heacham
● Great Snoring

● New Houghton
Hickling ●
Coltishall ●
KINGS LYNN ■
Horning ●
Potter Heigham
● Castle Acre
NORWICH ■

N O R F O L K

Nene

Little Ouse
A11
Thorpe ●

● Helpston
Barnack
● Stilton
● Little Gidding

Great Ouse

C A M B R I D G E S H I R E
● Coveney
Mildenhall
● Aldreth
● Wicken

S U F F O L K
Walberswick ●

● Hemingford Grey
A45
Swaffham Prior
CAMBRIDGE
● Grantchester ● Trumpington
BURY ST EDMUNDS ■
● Saxtead Green
Wickham ● Snape
Market ● Blaxhall

Cavendish
● Long Melford
Stoke-by-Clare ●
Stour
IPSWICH ■

● Wendens Ambo
● Great Cornard
Stoke by Nayland
East
Bergholt
Stratford St Mary ● Dedham

● Finchingfield

E S S E X
COLCHESTER ■
St
Osyth
A12

High Roding
Tolleshunt
D'Arcy
Aythorpe Roding
White Roding ● Leaden Roding
Abbess Roding ● Good Easter
Berners Roding ● Margaret Roding
Blackwater
CHELMSFORD

M11
Roding

ENGLISH CHANNEL

Thames
● Great Wakering

with timber-framed cottages among acres of ploughed fields and grazing land. **White Roding**, **High Roding** and **Leaden Roding** are the largest of them (though that is not saying much) and **Abbess Roding, Margaret Roding, Aythorpe Roding** and **Berners Roding** make up the family, with their charmingly named neighbour **Good Easter** nearby. In these and other parts of lowland England, where the farmland is predominantly arable, village pubs are more likely to be called the 'Plough' and the 'Wheatsheaf' than in the pasture land of the uplands, where the 'Golden Fleece' and the 'Woolsack' are more in evidence.

Beyond the much-photographed village of **Wendens Ambo** and **Finchingfield** – the former with its church along a little country lane and the latter

Great Wakering, Essex. The church of this attractive village, which enjoys the distinction of being in the Guinness Book of Records as the driest spot in Britain.

Church and cottages at Wendens Ambo. A picturesque corner of one of the best known of Essex villages, near Saffron Walden. There are Roman bricks and Norman work in the church.

Dedham Lock and Mill. *Constable frequently painted aspects of Dedham village, and this view shows the mill which his father owned there.*

Cavendish, Suffolk. The church of St Mary with its neighbouring cottages beside the large green, in one of the county's most attractive villages.

Constable Country. A typical pastoral scene beside the River Stour at Dedham, Essex. This stretch of the river was familiar territory to the artist, who lived nearby.

with its church on a hilltop – is the valley of the Stour, and on the Essex side of the river is Dedham, whose church is to be seen in the paintings of John Constable, for this is the so-called 'Constable Country' where the artist grew up and studied nature and did much of his finest work. Several villages across the river in Suffolk are strongly associated with him – **East Bergholt, Stoke by Nayland, Stratford St Mary** – and this peaceful corner of England has changed relatively little since Constable spent his observant boyhood on the banks of the Stour.

Further upstream, however, is the relatively neglected territory of an equally great English painter, Thomas Gainsborough, who exerted a powerful influence on Constable. 'I fancy I see Gainsborough in every hedge and hollow tree', he wrote. It was near the village of **Great Cornard**, now a suburb of Sudbury, where he was born, that Gainsborough painted several of his best-known landscapes.

East Anglia has produced an amazing number of English landscape artists – 'amazing' because one would not expect the flat uninterrupted landscape of the eastern counties to have inspired and fed the visual imagination. Other East Anglian artists are chiefly from Norfolk, but in Suffolk the former fishing village of **Walberswick** is notable as the setting for so much of Wilson Steer's best work, and a colony of artists still works there.

Inland Suffolk is well represented by villages south of the county town of Bury St Edmunds, such as **Cavendish, Stoke-by-Clare** and **Long Melford**. Around Ipswich, are **Saxtead Green, Wickham Market** and **Little Wenham**, while **Mildenhall** in the west and **Snape** in the east have more specialised attractions. Cavendish is one of the county's most beautiful villages, its thatched and colour-washed cottages making a well known picturesque group with the church, behind a large and tidy green.

Long Melford lives up to its name, featuring a very long and wide street flanked by a variety of fine

Melford Hall, Suffolk. The Tudor manor house, built when Elizabeth became queen, stands among much distinguished architecture in the stylish village of Long Melford.

buildings, with its large parish church at the top. The village was divided between several manors in medieval times, and two fine Tudor manor houses are among the village's proudest buildings, both built of brick. One is called Melford Hall and the other Kentwell Hall, the latter being a little outside the village and having what is said to be the largest dovecote in Suffolk.

The ambitious size of Suffolk's village churches, often built of flint with stone or brick dressings (for flint is the only natural building material available in the region), is accounted for by the wealth which accumulated in the hands of merchants and clothiers in the medieval wool trade. Long Melford's Holy Trinity church is big enough to be a cathedral, and is exceeded in impressiveness only by St Mary's at Mildenhall, a stately and fascinating village church with a superbly carved hammerbeam roof, a noble 113 foot (34.3 m) tower, and a seven-light east window of original design. Mildenhall has another claim to fame, for here in 1942, at Thistley Green, was uncovered the buried hoard of silver Roman tableware known as the Mildenhall Treasure, now on display in the British Museum.

Little Wenham is notable for its thirteenth-century fortified manor house, Little Wenham Hall. It is one of the earliest brick buildings in Suffolk, and its battlemented tower looks as much like a small castle, or indeed a church, as a house, but it was built at a time when lords of manors were no longer residing in castles and had to obtain licence from the king to give their homes reasonable defences against attack in unquiet times and unsettled areas.

The most interesting building at **Saxtead Green** is not the church, nor the manor house, but the windmill – a large and fully restored eighteenth-century post mill with a sail span of 155 feet (52.9 m). Harnessing the wind as a free source of power always made good sense in these windswept flatlands, and still would today. (A recent researcher on consumer goods was surprised to find that women in East Anglia still wore vests, but this ought to be no surprise in an area where winds blow unimpeded straight across the North Sea from the Ural Mountains of Siberia.)

Another characteristic type of building from this region is the old malthouse, with the familiar triangular cowl on top of its drying kiln, and the village 'maltings', as they are called, are what have made Snape known far beyond the immediate locality. Part of the nineteenth-century complex here has been converted into a fine modern concert hall, where part of the Aldeburgh Festival takes place. This annual festival of music was founded by the composer Benjamin Britten after the Second World War, and brings music lovers from far and wide to this relatively unknown corner of Suffolk where a fine riverside walk along the Alde links Aldeburgh itself with the village farther inland. Snape's church is almost as far north of the village centre as the maltings are south of it.

Near Snape is **Blaxhall**, an old agricultural village not especially pretty in appearance, but important as one of the chief sources of oral local history gathered so impressively by George Ewart Evans. Newcomers to the village, as he has recorded, are observed with suspicion until the old saying is confirmed: 'Only the rum 'uns come to Blaxhall'. But humans are not the only 'rum 'uns' here. A sandstone boulder in the yard of Stone Farm is the subject of local lore which maintains, despite all geological evidence to the contrary, that it was about the size of two fists when it was first found, and that it has steadily grown to its present five-ton (5.1 tonnes) weight.

The windmill at Saxtead Green. This fine early eighteenth-century post mill, with its four sails and fantail, is characteristic of east Suffolk mills.

Moving into Norfolk along the eastern coastal region, we are in the area east of Norwich which includes the Broads, where villages such as **Hickling**, **Coltishall**, **Horning** and **Potter Heigham** are characteristic, all providing facilities for holidaymakers afloat. The Broads were evidently created by centuries of digging for peat in this low-lying region of England, and one of the local industries which has resulted from the presence of these sheets of marshy water linked by streams and rivers is the growing and harvesting of reeds, the material with which so many village dwellings are roofed. The Norfolk reed or 'spear' is the best material for thatching, and a well-made roof here may last up to 80 years, which is why more thatched houses, cottages, pubs and other buildings survive in Norfolk and Suffolk than in other parts of the country.

The landscape artists of Norfolk were centred on the county capital and thus became known as the Norwich School of painters, but the villagers around the city were well represented by them, particularly **Thorpe**, on the River Yare, which is now an eastern suburb of the city. This high-class residential village provided subjects for John Crome and John Sell Cotman, the leading lights of what was the only genuine regional school of painting in the history of English art.

Castle Acre, to the north west, is host to art of a different kind. William de Warenne, son-in-law of William the Conqueror, was lord of the manor here, and he built a castle beside an ancient trackway from where the village grew. Hardly anything of the castle remains except the impressive earthworks, but Warenne also founded here a Cluniac priory,

Horning, Norfolk. A typical village of the Norfolk Broads, it stands by the River Bure, and is a popular centre for boating holidays.

A thatcher at work. Using Norfolk reeds, grown around the Broads, the thatcher re-roofs a house in his individual style – in this case with shaped tiers.

Castle Acre Priory. Norfolk's most impressive medieval remains are the stone and flint ruins of the Cluniac Priory founded by William the Conqueror's son-in-law.

and the ruins of this are among the most impressive medieval remains in East Anglia, particularly the west front of the priory church with its splendid Norman arcading.

New Houghton originated in the early eighteenth-century, when Sir Robert Walpole, the Georgian Prime Minister, built his vast Houghton Hall, demolishing the existing village to make way for his park – an essential appendage to every self-respecting landlord's house in those days. At least he provided new homes for the evicted villagers, building this small community of two-storey white-washed cottages in two rows of five leading to the south gates of the mansion.

Older villages and hamlets have more traditional local names, like **Dumpling Green, Great Snoring** and **Cley-next-the-Sea.** Dumpling Green was the birthplace of George Borrow, the original and extraordinary traveller, linguist and author of *Lavengro* and *Romany Rye*, who belongs to that group of English writers including Izaak Walton, Gilbert White, W.H.Hudson and George Ewart Evans, who have kept rural literature alive in the face of almost overwhelming competition from urban civilisation.

Great Snoring is an attractive village beside the River Stiffkey, and appropriately sleepy, though neither of its best buildings, the brick parsonage built by Sir Ralph Shelton as his manor house in the time of Henry VIII, and the church with its warning images of Death, Judgement, Heaven and Hell, is such as to induce snores. Cley-next-the-Sea is also a misnomer nowadays, for the place is actually a mile (1.6 km) inland, due to seventeenth-century land reclamation along the coast. The older guide books refer to this stranded port's church of St Margaret, with its ruined or never-completed transepts, but the best known building there today is the photogenic windmill. Cley, incidentally, is pronounced 'Cly' locally.

Burnham Thorpe is where Horatio Nelson was born, in 1758. Legend has it that his mother's contractions began when she was going for a drive in a pony-and-trap, and unable to reach home, she gave birth to her son in a barn near the inn of this village where his father was rector. Be that as it may, all the villages in the locality are justly proud of their national hero, as pubs such as 'The Nelson', 'The Trafalgar' and 'The Victory' make clear.

Pub signs are less noteworthy than village signs in Norfolk, however. Many of the attractive signs seen as one enters the villages of this area were made by Harry Carter, whose cousin Howard was the archaeologist who found the tomb of Tutankhamun in Egypt. One of the most unexpected signs in the whole county is to be found at **Heacham**, near Hunstanton, for it shows Pocahontas, the daughter of a Red Indian chief. What is she doing here beside the Wash? Well, she was married to John Rolfe of Heacham Hall, who had gone out to Virginia early in the seventeenth-century and brought her back to his family home where she gave birth to a son, Tom. She was on the point of returning to her native land when she died, aged only twenty-two, but Tom

The village sign at Heacham, Norfolk, which depicts the unlikely figure of Pocahontas, a Red Indian princess who was married to a local gentleman.

Cley-next-the-Sea, Norfolk. The brick-built windmill is of the tower type. Unlike post mills, only the cap, which carries the sails, turns in the wind.

Barnack, Cambridgeshire. The church tower was built in Saxon times, when the village had already long been noted for its building stone, quarried up to the nineteenth century.

went back later, and is said to have been the ancestor of several well known Americans, including President Woodrow Wilson's first wife.

Moving inland south westward from the Wash brings us to Cambridgeshire and the Fens. This is a large area of former marshland which has been reclaimed from the sea by centuries of drainage started by the Romans. The greatest names associated with the drainage of the fens are the fourth Earl of Bedford, who provided the money, and the Dutch engineer Cornelius Vermuyden, who supplied the expertise. In the seventeenth century great work was done here to claim valuable farmland from the sea, and names such as Bedford Level and New Bedford River are still to be found on the maps of the region, where fields and roads between the isolated villages are defined not by the fences, stone walls or hawthorn hedges to be seen elsewhere, but by low banks and ditches. Although as a general rule eastern England has more 'green' villages than the west, there are few in this area, where a village green would be a waste of the fertile soil so hard-won over a period of nearly 2000 years.

Coveney and **Aldreth**, near Ely, are typical tiny settlements which once stood on islands above the floodwaters, and are now reached by roads that seem to lead nowhere. **Wicken** is better known, for near this village is the National Trust nature reserve of Wicken Fen, the only fen which has been left more or less in its original condition – an undrained remnant of what the whole of the fenland region was like once – where the inhabitants, known to outsiders as 'fen slodgers', earned their livings by catching fish (especially eels) and waterfowl for the town markets. As drainage and the growing of crops takes the surplus water out of the soil, the other fens are slowly sinking, as is proved by the Holme Fen post near Peterborough. This was a cast iron pillar driven 22 feet (6.6 m) through the peat in 1851. It was almost buried originally, but now stands about 14 feet (4.2 m) above ground level.

Cambridgeshire is a county of great variety, particularly since the boundary changes which gave it Huntingdonshire and the Soke of Peterborough. Its villages include **Stilton**, which gave its name, rather by accident than design, to the finest and most famous of English cheeses; and **Little Gidding**, which T.S.Eliot commemorates in the last of his *Four Quartets* as a place 'where prayer has been valid', for here, in 1625, Nicholas Ferrar founded a community dedicated to prayer and good works.

Near the Suffolk border west of Newmarket is **Swaffham Prior**, a village where the chief interest lies in its two churches, St Mary's and St Cyriac's,

Wicken Fen, Cambridgeshire. The National Trust owns this smock mill, once used for pumping water in the drainage of the Fens. It stands near Wicken village, and can be visited.

Grantchester, Cambridgeshire. The village immortalised by Rupert Brooke, who left an indelible image of honey for tea at three o'clock on summer afternoons amid the rose gardens.

that stand side by side in the same churchyard. Each has a fine octagonal tower, and before the latter became largely derelict, they rivalled each other in size and magnificence. The village was split between two manors, neither of whose lords intended to be outdone by the other in his show of Christian piety and his claim to a place in the queue at the pearly gates.

Hemingford Grey is a picturesque village on the Great Ouse, with houses of brick, timber and thatch, and a manor house which has a strong claim to being the oldest manor house still inhabited in Britain. It is near the church, which stands at a bend in the river lined by willow trees. The willows are not pollarded, but the church steeple is, for its top was blown off by a storm in the eighteenth century

and all that remains is an unbecoming stump on the square tower. At about the time of this catastrophe, a human tragedy was enveloping the family of the manor house, which was then the home of two sisters, Maria and Elizabeth Gunning, the beautiful daughters of an Irish squire. Both were married in the same year, one to an earl, the other to a duke, but their happiness was short-lived. Maria died at twenty-seven from lead poisoning in her cosmetics, and Elizabeth was widowed six years after her marriage.

Trumpington and **Grantchester**, situated close together just outside Cambridge, have strong associations with a whole galaxy of English writers from Chaucer to E.M.Forster. The villages are a pleasant walking distance from the university town, though a more leisurely approach is by punt up the river. Wordsworth, Byron, Tennyson and Rupert Brooke among other writers have celebrated this locality in their verse. Brooke lodged at Grantchester in a room opening out on to 'a stone verandah covered with creepers, and a little old garden full of old-fashioned flowers and *crammed* with roses,' and his famous lines about the church clock striking three and was there 'honey still for tea?' also relate to Grantchester.

A poet of more parochial habit and origins was John Clare, who was born at the little village of **Helpston** in a cottage next door to the 'Blue Bell Inn'. The village was in Northamptonshire then, and Clare called it 'a gloomy village'. His father was a farm labourer and his mother a shepherd's daughter, and all his life – most of it spent here until he descended into disillusion and madness – Clare wrote about the things he had grown up with in this locality. He was a poet of nature who, like Constable, could make his life's work out of the spot where he was born, for:

While learned poets rush to bold extremes,
And sunbeams snatch to light the muse's fires,
An humble rustic hums his lowly dreams,
Far in the swale where poverty retires,
And sings what nature and what truth inspires.

Close to Helpston is the village of **Barnack**, one of the most important quarrying villages in England during the Middle Ages. It supplied stone for many village churches hereabouts, as well as for greater buildings much farther afield. The limestone for Ely and Peterborough cathedrals came from Barnack, as well as being used in Cambridge, Norwich and Rochester, among other places. The stone had first been worked by the Romans, but the seams were finally exhausted in the eighteenth century, and the site of the last quarrying carried out at Barnack, a humpy landscape covered with undergrowth, is known locally as 'Hills and Holes'. The village – pretty at its centre despite extremely off-putting brick and concrete buildings at its outskirts – is an ideal point from which to leave East Anglia and enter the North Midlands.

Hemingford Grey, Cambridgeshire. A delightful village on the River Ouse, its abbreviated church spire overlooks one of Britain's oldest inhabited manor houses.

Well dressing at Tissington, Derbyshire. This regional speciality is said to date from the time of the Black Death, but may be older. Flower petals form the decorations.

THE NORTH MIDLANDS

STONE is the key to the village character of much of the north Midlands. Moving into Lincolnshire from the area around Barnack, we are in the heart of the region's stone country, in the villages near Stamford, where quarrying of the limestone for building has been a local preoccupation for many centuries.

Lincolnshire's own stone villages stretch northward from Stamford on either side of a ridge known as Lincoln Edge, and **Edenham** and **Greatford** are among them, though very different from each other. Greatford is a spacious village of grey stone with a stone bridge crossing the River Glen and leading to the village church with its broach spire,

one of the characteristic features of east Midland churches. Edenham, on the other hand, is much more formal. It is an estate village built by the lords of the manor of nearby **Grimsthorpe**, where the modernised medieval castle is still occupied.

A huge number of villages in this eastern part of the Midlands have the '-by' name ending which signifies foundation during the Danish occupation, and most of those on Lincolnshire's stone belt – **Haceby, Braceby, Welby, Kelby** and **Oasby** – are attractive places with mostly stone houses roofed in the suddenly apparent red pantiles used northward from here throughout eastern England.

The creamy stone which looks so warm and happy beneath these red roofs generally came from **Ancaster** – a large village not beautiful in itself but the cause of beauty in others, such as Fulbeck, which is perhaps Lincolnshire's prettiest village. Its hilltop church built of Ancaster limestone, standing

Fulbeck, Lincolnshire. A highly attractive village of pale limestone walls and red pantile roofs on the ridge of high ground known as Lincoln Edge.

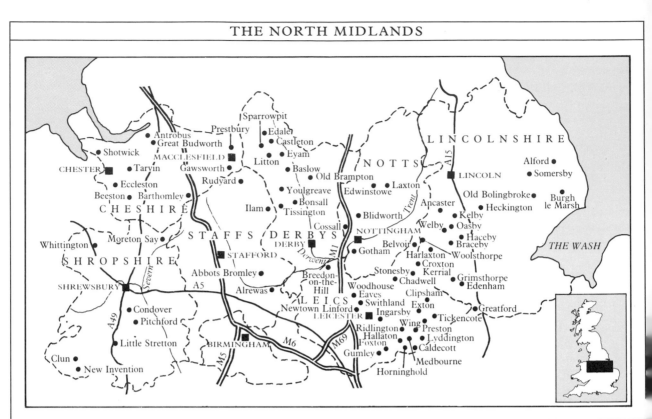

by the green, sports pinnacles and gargoyles, and overlooks the village street which runs gently down the hill to the valley of the River Witham.

Further east, on the Lincolnshire Wolds, is **Old Bolingbroke**, where only earthworks mark the site of the castle where Henry IV was born. The fortress was a Royalist stronghold in the Civil War, and after the Parliamentary victory in a battle at Winceby, nearby, the castle was demolished by order of Cromwell's local committee.

Somersby, a little to the north, was the birth-place of Alfred Lord Tennyson, whose father was the village rector, and there is a bust of the Poet Laureate in the church. Tennyson's father was an elder son who was disinherited in favour of his younger brother. The remains of Bayons Manor, which the poet's uncle built with pseudo-baronial megalomania at Tealby in the nineteenth century (having discovered or invented an ancient French family lineage), were blown up some years ago, but the village itself is a most attractive one.

An even more extravagant palace is situated at **Harlaxton**, the baroque manor house of George de Ligne Gregory, but far from being in ruins, it houses the University of Evansville, from Indiana. This vast mock-Tudor pile was built in the 1830s, but looks like some lavish film set abandoned by Metro-Goldwyn-Mayer.

Harlaxton Manor. This architectural extravaganza,

Nearer the Lincolnshire coast, where the land levels out to what most people imagine to be the whole county's flat landscape, windmills as well as church steeples lend their shapes to the skyline, and **Alford** has one with five sails. There is no law of God or Nature which says that four is the proper number of sails for a windmill, and Lincolnshire's millwrights have followed their own Nonconformist course in their buildings. A preserved mill at **Heckington**, near Sleaford, has eight sails, while at **Burgh le Marsh**, an outbuilding of the more conventional tower mill has been converted into an interesting windmill museum.

Laws of nature were the lifetime preoccupation of a famous son of Lincolnshire who was born at **Woolsthorpe**, in the manor house now preserved by the National Trust. Isaac Newton's mother, Hanna, gave birth to him on Christmas Day, 1642, and said he was so small that she could have cradled him in a quart mug. But he grew to be a giant in intellect. The guide book tale that an apple tree in the garden is descended from the one that shed its fruit on Sir Isaac's head continues the famous, but improbable legend, for it seems unlikely that a man of his genius would need such prompting to awaken fresh ideas.

Crossing over from Lincolnshire into Leicestershire, we are in what was formerly England's smallest county, Rutland, and arguably one of its prettiest. This is stone country again, where many of the villages are built of the Liassic limestone coloured brown by iron in the rock, which we first noticed in Northamptonshire, but used in conjunction with the finer-grained Oolitic limestone, it creates a complete colour contrast at places such as **Clipsham**, where the village quarries are still being worked after at least 700 years. They contributed the creamy stone to the attractive village houses as well as to more distant and somewhat grander edifices, the House of Commons and Buckingham Palace.

Almost every village in this area has something of interest for the tourist to see. 'Oo, a couldn't tell ya, me duck', said a lady of whom I asked directions to

built in the 1880s, is one of Lincolnshire's most spectacular buildings, in which limestone from Ancaster was used.

Lyddington, a village well worth seeking out for its historic Bede House, the former home of the Bishops of Lincoln, with a superb great hall and richly carved oak ceiling. **Tickencote** is well known to church enthusiasts for its spectacular Norman chancel arch. At **Exton**, the church in the park contains magnificent monuments to the Noels and Haringtons who lived here, by sculptors such as Grinling Gibbons and Nollekens. In **Wing**, an ancient turf maze is preserved, on which village children used to perform a ceremony called 'Troy

Tickencote, Leicestershire. The Norman chancel arch in the church of St Peter is among the more fantastic village sights in the former tiny county of Rutland.

Town' on Easter Mondays, recalling some long-forgotten Celtic ritual.

Preston, Caldecott and **Ridlington** are all attractive villages of ironstone, which continues to be used into old Leicestershire at **Hallaton, Horninghold** and several smaller places such as **Foxton** and **Gumley**. Hallaton is one of the largest villages in this corner of the county and is full of intimations of pagan influence. Easter Monday rituals are still observed here, to the occasional embarrassment of the village rector, who is required to supply a hare pie which is broken up and scrambled for in a kind of symbolic rape in which the hare represents a witch and the participants devils. A 'bottle-kicking' game with the neighbouring village of **Medbourne** follows this routine: the bottles or casks containing ale are drunk at the conical market cross to the accompaniment of a brass band and the monotonous tune of a church clock, which chimes every three hours, day and night.

Foxton is of more practical interest. Between it and Gumley there is a hill which obstructed the route of the proposed Leicestershire and North-

amptonshire Union Canal in 1793. This problem, together with enormous costs, brought the whole project to a temporary halt, and when it was revived by the newly formed Grand Union Canal Company, Thomas Telford suggested building an ambitious flight of locks instead of tunnelling through the hillside. Ten locks raised the water level by 75 feet (22.7 m), taking coal-laden barges over the hill instead of through it. They were regarded as one of the engineering triumphs of the period, and the Foxton Staircase is now a popular destination for local afternoon drives.

Ingarsby, to the east of Leicester, is well signposted, but the village has vanished. It had gone by 1469, when Leicester Abbey acquired the manor and destroyed the village to create pasture for sheep.

The turf maze at Wing, Leicestershire. A small number of these mazes survives, in various parts of England. They are extremely ancient, and are often known as 'Troy Town'.

Ingarsby is a classic example of those lost medieval villages which have been traced throughout the country by dedicated researchers in recent years. Only a high bumpy field, which cannot be ploughed because of stone foundations beneath the soil, tells where village houses and streets were once inhabited by the men, women and children who were driven out by the sheep.

In the northern part of Leicestershire, the Wolds are the territories of the aristocratic Quorn and Belvoir Hunts. Foxhunting on an organised basis seems to have been started at the beginning of the eighteenth century, and had its origins in Leicestershire, where Thomas Boothby and Hugo Meynell are credited with its establishment as a properly conducted upper-class sport. Villages such as

Alford Mill. Lincolnshire's village millwrights were nothing if not independent, and the one who built this tower mill in the nineteenth century gave it five sails.

Hallaton, Leicestershire. The curiously shaped market cross stands on the green of the old county's prettiest village, surrounded by cottages of ironstone, many of them thatched.

Croxton Kerrial and **Belvoir** (the first pronounced 'Crowston' and the second 'Beaver') have strong associations with hunting, as does the beautiful Vale of Belvoir, but here the quarry is destined to change from fox to coal. A long campaign to prevent mining in the Vale has predictably failed, and stone-built country villages such as **Stonesby** and **Chadwell** now live under the shadow of approaching industry. One of the heroes of the opposition to this development has been the Duke of Rutland, whose home, Belvoir Castle, is one of Leicestershire's great tourist attractions.

Industry and red brick building feature throughout most of the flatter western half of Leicestershire, except in the area of Charnwood Forest, where villages such as **Newtown Linford**, **Swithland** and **Woodhouse Eaves** grace a romantic landscape in the middle of a territory of coal mining and hosiery factories. Ancient granite occurs here, and village houses are often built of it and roofed in the multi-tinted Swithland slate which was quarried for many centuries in the area. The country chur-

chyards contain headstones of the same material, which lent itself to precise and elaborate engraving and was fully exploited by the local craftsmen.

One village which must be seen by church enthusiasts is **Breedon-on-the-Hill**, in the county's north west corner. At the top of a winding road from the main street, where the old village lock-up still stands, is the ancient church, perched on a cliff-top like an eagle watching all that goes on below. Inside it are fragments of eighth-century Saxon carving depicting strange birds and beasts. It is a common village legend throughout England, where churches are isolated or hard to reach, that the medieval masons started to build the church on a different spot – in this case at the foot of the hill – but every morning found their stones had been moved elsewhere during the night. It is easy to understand the superstitions of simple country folk of former times when faced with unfamiliar images they could not understand, such as those at Breedon, which look like creatures of the Devil rather than of God, being birds and beasts unknown in Noah's Ark.

Neither Staffordshire nor Shropshire is especially noted for attractive villages, but travelling westward, we do begin to notice the building speciality for which the west Midlands is famous – black-and-white timber-framed houses. The northern half of Shropshire, lying across the flat Midland Plain, is a veritable study in black-and-white, with its half-timbered buildings, Friesian cattle and a multitude of magpies.

Moreton Saye was the birthplace of Clive of India, but between that event and his burial here, so many travels, adventures, misdeeds, trials and tribulations were packed into a life lasting less than fifty years that it is very difficult to associate this little place with such a worldly figure. The English villages have supplied this country with so many of its great men, but too often the towns and cities claim them after death and we know little of the influence upon them of their rural upbringing.

One of the finest black-and-white houses in this region is at **Pitchford**, where a Shrewsbury wool

Ingarsby, Leicestershire. Aerial photography reveals the layout and foundations of a village of which nothing is visible at ground level. It was deserted in the fifteenth century.

Foxton Locks, Leicestershire. The so-called 'Foxton Staircase' of ten locks was Telford's answer to a problem of canal engineering. It lifts narrow-boats 75 feet over a hill.

Clun Castle, Shropshire. One of the countless castle ruins of the Welsh Marches, it stands above the village since reckoned one of the 'quietest under the sun'.

Pitchford Hall, Shropshire. A fine timber-framed mansion characteristic of the west Midland counties, though superior to most, it was built around 1570 for a rich wool merchant.

merchant, Adam Otley, built Pitchford Hall in the sixteenth century. It is a model of symmetrical restraint, displaying none of the Elizabethan flamboyance which spoils so many large houses of the kind elsewhere (the house is not open to the public, but it can be glimpsed from the road through the village).

At **Condover**, is Condover Hall, a Tudor mansion of very different appearance, built of sandstone, that is now a school for the blind. This village was the birthplace of Richard Tarleton, the favourite comedian of Elizabeth I, and probably the inspiration for Shakespeare's 'poor Yorick', whom Hamlet calls 'a fellow of infinite jest'.

The hills of south Shropshire – the 'blue remembered hills' of Housman's *A Shropshire Lad* – support many small and scattered farming communities, and almost as many ruined castles along the Welsh Marches which were for so many centuries an unsettled borderland of intermittent raiding and plundering. Almost every village had its castle at one time, and many still have impressive remains, such as **Clun** and **Whittington**. There is a

hamlet in Shropshire's borderland called **New Invention**, and local wags are inclined to tell you that it gets its name from a village blacksmith of long ago, who had the idea of fitting horseshoes on backwards so that the Welsh would think from their tracks that the enemy was retreating, not advancing.

It was A. E. Housman who brought a local quartet to the nation's notice:

> Clunton and Clunbury,
> Clungunford and Clun,
> Are the quietest places
> Under the sun.

But the locals had other and less flattering endings to the verse before the professor adapted it for his own poetic purposes.

Shropshire natives use 'like' ('loike') a lot, in a sense which seems to betray a not-surprising lack of security, stuck as they are between Wales and Birmingham; and you may catch an older villager using 'her' instead of 'she': 'Her 'ad lovely long 'air when 'er were a kid, loike.'

In the long gap formed by a geological fault

Abbots Bromley Horn Dance. This famous Staffordshire ritual is pre-Norman in origin, and has some meaning lost in antiquity. Its survival indicates the power of rural tradition.

between the Long Mynd and the Stretton Hills, **Little Stretton** is notable for its pretty black-and-white church with thatched roof, near one of the well known beauty spots of the area – Ashes Hollow.

Although picturesque villages in Staffordshire are few and far between, **Alrewas** and **Rudyard** deserve mention in any book on the subject. Alrewas is a quiet little place near Lichfield, with magpie cottages beneath thatched roofs, where the occupants were once preoccupied with basket weaving. The Trent and Mersey Canal passes through the village, and there is an old cotton mill there too. Rudyard, north of Stoke-on-Trent, is an attractive village near a reservoir which was made for supplying water to the canal, and which offers boating and fishing facilities. Romantic notion has it that John Lockwood Kipling proposed to Alice Macdonald here, and when their son was born in India two years later, they named him after the place. It is not often pointed out that Rudyard was actually the writer's second Christian name. His first was Joseph, after his grandfather.

Abbots Bromley was a market town once, but is now hardly more than a large village, and it owes its fame to the ancient Horn Dance performed here in September by a team of twelve. Six men wear the reindeer antlers which are stored in the church throughout the year, and they are accompanied by two musicians, a man on a hobby horse, and a man with a crossbow, Maid Marian and a jester, all dressed in medieval costume. The ritual is pre-Norman in origin, and involves a symbolic conflict between light and darkness, among other things. It is performed repeatedly throughout the day at various points over a wide area round the village.

Ilam, in Dovedale, is an untypical but most interesting place, largely built by George Gilbert Scott for the nineteenth-century lord of the manor, Jesse Watts Russell. It has uniform brown, tile-hung gabled cottages with ground floors of stone, a saddleback-towered church, and the Izaak Walton Hotel beside the River Manifold – for this area was well known to Walton and his friend Charles Cotton, as well as to Samuel Johnson. No visitor to Ilam should be so carried away by its scenery and literary associations that he misses seeing the fine monument in the church to David Pike Watts, Russell's father-in-law, by Sir Francis Chantrey.

Cheshire's villages include **Eccleston**, a dignified estate village of the Dukes of Westminster near Chester, with some black-and-white building; and **Beeston**, where the clifftop ruins of the Earl of Chester's castle offer spectacular views of the Cheshire Plain far below. Neither village can be called typical of this county where black-and-white building has to share its glory with red sandstone (used particularly for churches) and a great deal of brick.

In fact, Cheshire is a county of relatively few villages of any kind, but one of the best of them is **Prestbury**, on the River Bollin. It remains attractive despite modern development, and has in the churchyard of St Peter's, a little Norman chapel which is all that remains of the original church here.

The occasional bad local habit of painting a black-and-white half-timbered effect upon brick or even stone walls might have earned some ridicule from one of the county's most famous sons, Charles Lutwidge Dodgson, better known as Lewis Carroll, if he had stayed there long enough, but although he was born at **Newton-by-Daresbury** where his father was vicar of the parish, he left the county when he was eleven. The village church commemorates him, all the same, in a window showing him in the company of his creations – the White Rabbit, the Mad Hatter, the March Hare and, of course, Alice.

There is a little of the nonsensical about **Gawsworth**, which is among the county's most visited places, and quite unique. The Fitton family were lords of the manor for over 300 years, and Mary Fitton, who went to court and had an affair with William Herbert, Earl of Pembroke – much to the displeasure of Queen Elizabeth – is supposed by some to have been the 'dark lady' of Shakespeare's sonnets. At any rate, Gawsworth Hall, the family's home, was a half-timbered mansion until the eighteenth century, when it was partly refaced in brick, with the black-and-white effect incongruously painted on. It occupies a picturesque site among trees and pools in a village with other interesting buildings and, nearby, Maggoty Johnson's Wood, named after England's last professional jester, who lived at the hall for a time.

Shotwick and **Barthomley** are quietly attractive villages. The former has a fine church with a massive tower, and the latter retains its rural

Gawsworth, Cheshire. The many Fitton monuments in the church of St James commemorate a local family whose members may have included Shakespeare's 'dark lady' of the sonnets.

Ilam Hall, Staffordshire. The home of the Watts Russell family, it was originally larger

and more spectacular. It is now a National Trust property used as a youth hostel.

tranquillity in spite of the M6 motorway thundering past its back door. But both these villages only just make it into Cheshire, teetering on the borders of Clwyd and Staffordshire respectively.

More securely situated are the neighbouring villages of **Antrobus** and **Great Budworth**: where Oak Apple Day has an uncomfortable significance for children who fail to observe it, for if they go to school on 29 May without a sprig of oak in their buttonholes they are liable to have their legs beaten by the other children with stinging nettles. A less aggressive custom is kept up at some other villages, such as **Tarvin**, where the church bell is rung at 11 o'clock on Shrove Tuesday to signal the start of pancake frying.

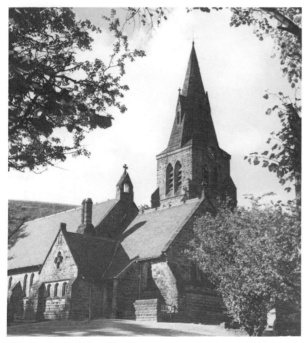

Edale, Derbyshire. Carboniferous sandstone, or 'Millstone Grit', imparts a northern ruggedness to this village church at the southern end of the Pennines below the Peak.

Derbyshire's best known tradition is well dressing, which is carried out in several Peak District villages, notably **Litton, Bonsall, Youlgreave** and **Tissington**, usually on Ascension Day. The custom is said to derive from medieval times when the purity of the limestone springs preserved the locality from the worst ravages of the Black Death. Others say that the springs never ran dry during the great drought of 1615 when no rain fell for four months.

However apocryphal that story may be, some of these villages deserve notice for other more valid reasons. Tissington, in particular is often cited as Derbyshire's most beautiful village and is a dazzling place of pale limestone houses – enriched in autumn by Virginia creeper and yellow lichen – around a duckpond and spacious village greens. Litton is interesting for some curiously long and narrow fields bounded by dry-stone walls. They are survivals of the medieval open fields which were sold in strips to yeoman farmers who enclosed them, and in these days of prairie-like arable farmland with huge agricultural machinery, they make a rare sight. Their reverse-S shape is due to the manoeuvring of teams of oxen during medieval ploughing of the ridge-and-furrow strips.

What conceivable manoeuvring accounts for the idiosyncratic church clock at **Old Brampton**, near Chesterfield, is impossible to explain, for it is divided into 63 minutes. Was it merely a mathematical error, or a deliberate act of defiance by a Nonconforming Midlander determined to show his independence? Perhaps it was intended to recover the 11 days which rustic Englishmen were convinced had been stolen from their lives when the Gregorian calendar came into force in 1752.

This is very clearly stone country again. Many quarries are still active in Derbyshire, not so much for building stone nowadays but rather for crushed roadstone and the ground limestone used by chemical industries. **Castleton** and **Sparrowpit** are among the quarrying villages of wildly contrasting size, and are better known to most tourists as the sites of the great caves and potholes of the district, such as Eldon Hole and Peak Cavern.

Baslow and **Edale**, by the Derwent and the Noe respectively, are among many other beautifully situated villages that carry hints of northern ruggedness. **Eyam**, up on the moors, compels particular respect. This village was devastated by bubonic plague in the seventeenth century, when a box of infected clothes was delivered to the village tailor. Forty-five people were soon dead, but instead of fleeing for their lives, the remaining villagers were persuaded by their rector, William Mompesson, that their Christian duty lay in total isolation so that they did not spread the disease to other communities, and Eyam cut itself off from the world in an act of communal heroism. Two thirds of the population died, including Rev. Mompesson's wife Katherine, whose grave is in the churchyard, and the father and six children of a family named Hancock, leaving

Edwinstowe, Nottinghamshire. Winter landscape at the village in Sherwood Forest where Robin Hood is reputed to have married Maid Marian.

only the mother alive to bury them all herself in the open field. Food supplies for the living were left outside the village for collection and paid for with coins left in jars of vinegar, which was thought then to be a disinfectant.

Nottinghamshire's chief hero is Robin Hood, and although the natural habitat of him and his merry men was Sherwood Forest, **Edwinstowe**, a pretty village near the best remaining parts of the forest, claims strong associations with the legendary outlaw. He is said to have married Maid Marian in the village church, and the Major Oak near the village was a favourite rendezvous. Whether you believe in Robin Hood or not, the Major Oak is an awe-inspiring tree. It has a girth of 30 feet (9.1 m) and is reputed to be more than 1000 years old. Both Maid Marian and Will Scarlet are reputed to have come from **Blidworth**, an unromantic coal-mining village these days, farther south.

Cossall, near Ilkeston, is also in the coal-mining country where another famous rebel grew up, D.H.Lawrence. Born at Eastwood, he became engaged to Louise Burrows, who lived at Church Cottage in Cossall, but the romance did not last long, though Lawrence later modelled Ursula in *Women in Love* on her. The village is now a rural oasis surrounded by an industrial desert.

Nottinghamshire is not a county where one naturally seeks the picturesque, but it has great historical interest, beginning perhaps with **Laxton**, where the medieval practice of farming three large unenclosed fields in strips is still carried on. One field lies fallow each year, and the other two are divided into strips shared between the farmers. Of course, the farming is not done today as it was in the Middle Ages – there are no teams of oxen, for one thing – but the principle is the same, and Laxton's open fields are registered as an Ancient Monument.

Gotham, between Nottingham and the Leicestershire border, is an unprepossessing village of this mining county, yet it is known throughout the civilised world, on account of the 'Wise Men' who allegedly lived there in King John's time. Stories of the folly for which the village was noted were collected and written down at least as far back as the sixteenth century, and the most widely accepted explanation is that the villagers pretended to be mad in order to deter the king from putting a public highway through their village or building a hunting lodge there. The king's agents were greeted by men who were attempting to drown an eel in a pool of water, while others were building a wall high enough to prevent the cuckoos from escaping, so that it would be springtime all year round. One supposes that Jonathan Swift was familiar with these tales, for the scientists of the academy at Lagado, in *Gulliver's Travels*, are similarly engaged in ludicrous experiments, such as turning ice into gunpowder and extracting sunbeams from cucumbers.

Elsdon, Northumberland. The pele tower, designed for defence during border warfare, belonged to the vicar of the parish. It was built in the fourteenth century.

YORKSHIRE AND THE NORTH-EAST

It is debatable whether folly or heroism should be attributed to the rector of **Epworth**, in Humberside. He fathered nineteen children, but if he and his wife had decided that fourteen· was enough, we should not have had John Wesley, the founder of Methodism, nor indeed Charles, the celebrated Methodist preacher and hymn writer. The original rectory was burnt down by an angry mob hostile to the rector's political views and is now rebuilt. Nonconformist chapels have not featured much in this tour of English villages, since these tend to be a product of larger urban communities (zealous evangelists were too keen on converting large crowds to bother much with rural hamlets). But this was the birthplace of Methodism, which influenced poorer working people throughout the land, from the mining communities of Yorkshire to Cornwall, and here in the large village of Epworth stands the stone church, built in 1889, that is representative of all of them, situated in the characteristically bleak landscape that welcomed the hope Wesley offered.

Horkstow, over to the east, is the less well known scene of a more private event contemporary with the advent of Wesley. The artist George Stubbs rented an isolated farmhouse, since demolished, just outside this village and lived here amid the putrefying flesh of the horses that he carefully dissected in studies for his great work *The Anatomy of the Horse*, which is still a classic of scientific illustration.

Alkborough has earlier associations than either Stubbs or Wesley. Near the church is Julian's Bower, a turf maze cut in the ground like the one we noticed at Wing, though of different design and a little larger. A replica is cut into the stone floor of the church porch, probably in the belief that it would keep evil spirits at bay, whilst the design is also repeated in a stained glass window and on a headstone in the churchyard, where a village squire was buried in 1922. Thus pagan influence has been kept alive for centuries by the Christian church, for these spirals are Celtic symbols of magic.

Burton Agnes and **Burton Constable** are not, as one would suppose, near neighbours but are far apart in Humberside north of the great river. The former boasts the treasure of Burton Agnes Hall, an Elizabethan mansion of red brick with stone dressings, full of architectural adornment, rich furnishings and modern French paintings, as well as – according to legend – the skull of a daughter of the

Alkborough, Humberside. Christianity paradoxically embraces paganism in this tombstone as elsewhere in the village church, perhaps through misunderstanding of the maze's origin.

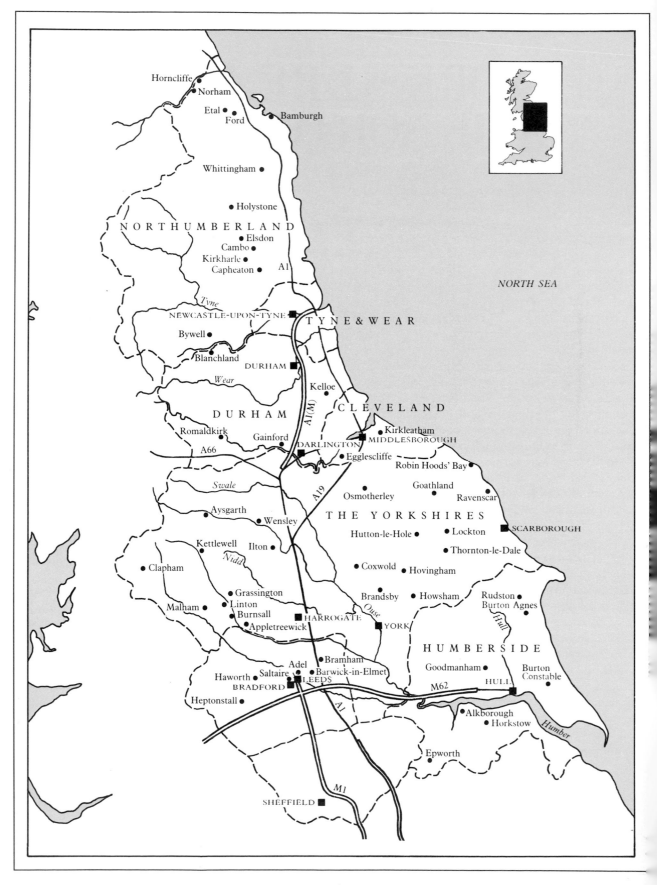

Burton Agnes Hall, Humberside. This magnificent red brick mansion was built in the early years of the seventeenth century by Sir Henry Griffith.

house. This was recovered from her coffin and buried in the walls after her dying wish had been ignored, resulting in her restless ghostly visitations to the house, for she had wished never to leave the place where she had been so happy. Burton Constable also has a great house in grounds laid out by Capability Brown, but no parallel romantic legend.

Goodmanham is the scene of a story in Bede's *Ecclesiastical History of the English Nation*. The venerable author tells us that Coifi, a high priest of the pagan religion, was converted to Christianity in AD 627, and personally led the destruction by fire of his own former temple. 'This place where the idols were is ... not far from York, to the eastward beyond the river Derwent, and is now called God-mundingham, where the high priest, by the inspiration of the true God, profaned and destroyed the altars which he had himself consecrated.' The village church of All Saints now stands on the spot.

Rudston, near Bridlington, has a more solid representative of paganism in its churchyard, in the form of a 25 foot (7.5 m) monolith erected here by men unknown to us and for reasons equally obscure. It is the tallest standing stone in Britain, and looks positively weird among the gravestones right beside the church. Local folklore accounts for it by saying that the Devil threw it to destroy the church, but just missed.

South and West Yorkshire might seem far too industrialised to offer anything worth while with regard to village England, but the enthusiastic seeker may find much of interest among the woollen mills, coal mines and iron foundries of the larger industrial conurbations. **Heptonstall**, for instance, is an industrial village, where weavers worked in their cottages before the powered mills came, but the factory industry stayed down in the valley at Hebden Bridge, leaving Heptonstall as a kind of fossilised weavers' village up on the hilltop. Built of the dark local stone made darker by the smoke of industry floating upwards to it, it has a sign marking the 'Top oth town', as well as a storm-ruined church paved with old gravestones, for this is a place familiar with death *en masse*. The Plague and the Civil War accounted for many lives in this village long ago. There are said to be 10,000 corpses in the graveyard and headstones have often been used twice.

Haworth had a high death-rate in the nineteenth century, and decomposing bodies in the churchyard gave health inspectors much cause for concern. If Heptonstall can be termed a town, it is hard to justify calling Haworth a village, but it is mentioned briefly here in deference to those who would be shocked if one of Yorkshire's most magnetic places were left out of a book such as this. It was a moorland village when the Brontës lived at the parsonage and the other villagers were mainly quarrymen and weavers. The weavers' cottages of Millstone grit still line the steep cobbled streets, with their long rows of windows in the upper

Heptonstall, West Yorkshire. A rugged northern hilltop village built of stone, where weavers worked in their cottages before the advent of factory industry.

Rudston, Humberside. The gigantic monolith in the village churchyard is Britain's tallest standing stone, set up like a phallic symbol long before the church was built beside it.

Wensley, North Yorkshire. The bridge over the Ure leads into a delightful stone-built village which gave its name to a fine cheese as well as to the dale it stands in.

Saltaire, West Yorkshire. A nineteenth-century engraving showing Sir Titus Salt's village, centred on his huge Alpaca wool mill, well outside Bradford, which now surrounds it.

Thornton-le-Dale. Thornton Beck pirouettes through one of the prettiest villages of north-east England, at the edge of the North York Moors.

storeys; and the 'Black Bull Inn' where Branwell Brontë drank himself to death is also still there.

Haworth's industrial growth has stretched it out to within a stone's throw of Bradford, and the city now engulfs a former village of some importance in the story of village England. **Saltaire** was built outside the city by Sir Titus Salt. As the first model village for industrial workers, it predated Port Sunlight and Bournville. The employees of Sir Titus Salt's palatial mill were housed there, away from the grime and smoke of Bradford, and he built them their own school, hospital, church, public baths and laundry, as well as a riverside park. Today it all still stands – a pioneering modern village which is now a city suburb.

Adel, now virtually enclosed by Leeds, barely hangs on to its former village character, but its tiny Norman church of St John the Baptist is popular with young city couples for their weddings, confirming that dream of rural England that resides somewhere in the unconscious of even the most resigned urban dweller. **Bramham**, to the east, has been rescued from disaster by the building of the A1 by-pass, for the busy trunk road was a great threat to this pale village of cream-coloured Magnesian limestone, with its red pantile roofs and stylish great house and gardens, Bramham Park. **Barwick-in-Elmet** near here, incidentally, is distinguished for having England's tallest permanent maypole, which stands 86 feet (29.1 m) high.

As we enter North Yorkshire, the need to be selective becomes increasingly difficult. This very large county boasts so much interest in its multitudinous villages it is almost an embarrassment

when space is limited, and those southerners who still, even in these days of easy communications, think that everywhere north of Birmingham is industry and grime, ought to be given a free day's coach tour in this area during which they would not set eyes on one factory chimney. Sadly there is insufficient scope here to cover places such as

The Brontë's church. St Michael's at Haworth, West Yorkshire, where Patrick Brontë preached his sermons and buried his son Branwell and his daughters Emily and Charlotte.

Shandy Hall, Coxwold. This is the farmhouse-cum-parsonage which Rev. Laurence Sterne named after his instantly-successful fictional character, Tristram Shandy.

Wensley and **Clapham**, **Lockton** and **Goathland**, **Hovingham** and **Grassington** – the traveller in Yorkshire will have to discover its villages for himself, and all I can do is to point him on his way.

Let me start with the picture postcard villages of the eastern half. **Thornton-le-Dale, Hutton-le-Hole** and **Coxwold** are pre-eminent among the limestone villages always dressed up in their Sunday best for visitors who come pouring off the 'mystery tour' coaches, as they do at Bourton-on-the-Water in the Cotswolds or Polperro in Cornwall. Each of these three might claim to be Yorkshire's prettiest village, but each has its own distinctive character. The distinctive character of Coxwold was the Rev. Laurence Sterne, author of the longest shaggy dog story in English literature, *The Life and Opinions of Tristram Shandy*. His home was a brick farmhouse which he called Shandy Hall, but he did not spend much time here during his eight years as village curate, for he was in demand in London society, and was buried there when he died. But like Thomas Hardy in far-away Dorset, he was not allowed to rest in peace. His corpse put in an unexpected appearance in Cambridge, where the Professor of Anatomy was about to dissect a specimen when someone recognised it as Laurence Sterne, and he was saved this indignity perpetrated by 'resurrection men'. In 1969 his body was removed from the graveyard at Bayswater, which was to be demolished, and his bones were finally (one hopes) laid to rest here in Coxwold churchyard.

In the Howardian Hills, **Brandsby** is noteworthy as the site of another of England's few surviving turf mazes. Many people believe these to be Christian in origin, but they are certainly older in idea, and can be traced with some confidence to the influence of ancient Greek rituals on the Celtic settlers in Britain.

Thornton-le-Dale has a twinkling beck which winds its way between stone cottages reached by little bridges and it has appeared on a multitude of chocolate boxes and calendars. Hutton-le-Hole has two becks meeting in a moorland dip where sheep graze freely on the wide village greens and bridges punctuate the scene of grey-walled cottages with pantile roofs, scattered along winding lanes.

On this side of North Yorkshire away from the Pennines is **Howsham**, a small and quiet village of toffee-coloured cottages where George Hudson, the 'Railway King', was born. He first went into his father's drapery business, until getting the magic touch of big business with the growth of the railway system. He became MP for Sunderland and was three times Lord Mayor of York before his disgrace, when it was discovered that he had fiddled the books.

It is strange that Yorkshire should be so hard on one robber and so proud of another, for it claims Robin Hood as one of its greatest sons, denying that Nottinghamshire was his true domain, and **Robin Hood's Bay** is perhaps circumstantial evidence – so named, it is sometimes said, because the Abbot of Whitby engaged him to rid the local coast of pirates. The village street swoops down to the stony shore at an alarming gradient, with a maze of cobbled alleys and flights of stone steps on either side, which local smugglers knew like the back of their hands when it came to escaping from the Excise men.

Between **Ravenscar** on the coast near here, and **Osmotherley**, on 't'other side o' t' moors', enthusiasts undertake the Lyke Wake Walk – a distance of 40 miles (64.3 km). If they can do it in 24 hours they can join the club at Osmotherley, where a stone slab on the green used to serve as a vegetable stall on market days and as a pulpit for John Wesley on his occasional visits. The long walk is named after the Lyke Wake Dirge, which launched the souls of the dead on their necessary journey across the moors:

> If ivver thoo gav owther bite or sup,
> Ivvery neet an' all,
> T'fleames'll nivver catch thee up,
> An' Christ tak up thy soul.

> But if bite or sup thoo nivver gav nean,
> Ivvery neet an' all,
> T'fleames'll bon thee sair to t'bean,
> An' Christ tak up thy soul.

The belief no doubt had its origins in some Viking lore, and seems a graphic incentive to the customary hospitality of Yorkshire folk.

Over on the Pennines, **Kettlewell** in Upper Wharfedale is a grey stone village in a rugged landscape, attracting rock climbers who come to tackle Great Whernside and Kilnsey Crag. Farther down the valley is a string of stone villages which

Hutton-le-Hole, North Yorkshire. A highly picturesque village of stone and pantile cottages, with greens, sheep and stream, which owes its existence to Quaker iron-mining interests.

Aysgarth Falls, North Yorkshire. The River Ure flows down Wensleydale and tumbles into Aysgarth via a series of these rocky cascades.

include **Linton**, once proclaimed 'loveliest village of the North'; **Burnsall**, another contender among widely dispersed claimants to the title of prettiest village in Yorkshire; and the delightfully named **Appletreewick**, which gives nothing away to its larger neighbours in intrinsic prettiness or superb siting, with Simon Seat rising on one side and Rylstone Fell on the other. Burnsall has a maypole on its green and Linton boasts an unexpectedly fine almshouse, Fountaine's Hospital, built, with uncompromising sex discrimination, for six poor women. The grandness of the hospital is accounted for by the fact that it was built by Vanbrugh – for Richard Fountaine, lord of the manor, was his timber merchant.

Less well known, perhaps, is the charitable work of the local squire at **Ilton**, an isolated hamlet on the moor above Masham. The persistent searcher may find here, well hidden by trees, a megalithic monument of startling completeness, with a grotto, several trilithons and a sacrificial table, all known as the Druids' Temple. Alas, the whole thing dates back no farther than the 1820s, when William Danby paid unemployed men a shilling a day to erect this splendid folly, rather than have them feeling ashamed to receive charity.

The Pennine rivers tumble through the dales between wild and lonely moors and occasionally water a village *en route* such as **Aysgarth**, where a mile of rocky river bed forms the turbulent Aysgarth Force, a popular spot for tourists with the River Ure cascading down a series of small falls.

How diminutive this beauty is, however, can be fully appreciated near the attractive village of **Malham** in Upper Airedale, where before the Ice Age, the spectacular curved limestone cliff known as Malham Cove had the River Aire tumbling over its edge into a 240 foot (72.9 m) waterfall. Now, the river trickles out somewhat sheepishly, from the foot of the cliff, and it is necessary to cross over into Durham for the nearest parallel remaining in England, High Force near Newbiggin, which is a mere 70 foot (21 m) drop.

Durham does not offer a lot in the way of picturesque English villages, any more than Cleveland or Tyne & Wear, but these counties should not be dismissed altogether on that account. **Gainford** and **Romaldkirk** must not be missed. The characteristic local long village greens are to be found here, lined with dignified houses of dark gritstone with some brick buildings and colour-washing among them. Gainford always belonged to Durham, but the county has won Romaldkirk from North Yorkshire in recent boundary changes, and may count itself very fortunate in that respect.

Kelloe, nearer Durham itself, was the birthplace of Elizabeth Barrett Browning, though the house, Coxhoe Hall, is no longer standing. She did not spend long here, as her since-notorious father moved the family to Herefordshire before going on to London's Wimpole Street, but this village must

Robin Hood's Bay, North Yorkshire. A quaint and fascinating coastal village associated in fact with smugglers and in legend with the famous outlaw.

have made some contribution to her character, however slight, and maybe more than a little to her father's.

The hard northern character is often reflected in the village names, so different and more down-to-earth than the lyrical names familiar in Somerset and Dorset, for instance. **Egglescliffe** and **Kirkleatham**, in Cleveland, might serve as examples, but the villages themselves are not as unyielding as their names suggest, for they both have much style. Egglescliffe, perched perilously on the very fringes of Stockton-on-Tees, and overlooking the river, does not even have a motor road through it.

Even Tyneside keeps a pleasant surprise or two up its sleeve. **Bywell**, just inside Northumberland, has been called 'the most picturesque and architecturally rewarding of all Tyneside villages'. It was a large village once, shared by two manors, and thriving on iron-working, naturally enough, but it has declined to little more than a hamlet now, although it has a manor house, two churches and the remains of a castle. The church of St Peter was called the 'black church' locally, because it belonged to the black-cowled monks of Benedictine Durham, and the church of St Andrew, belonging to the Premonstratensian canons of Blanchland, was the 'white church'.

Blanchland itself is one of the most delightfully surprising of all northern English villages. Not that it is pretty in the same way as Thornton-le-Dale and Clapham. Indeed, it was built as an industrial estate village by the Earl of Crewe, who was also Bishop of Durham, for workers in his lead mines, constructed out of the ruins of the abbey and the original village,

which had been in decline for 200 years, since the Dissolution. Wesley called the place a heap of ruins when he preached here in 1747, but its restoration began five years later, and it created a unique village, totally uncharacteristic, but with great dignity and even beauty of a sort. Its gravelled square with shops on one side seems to keep about it the quiet spirit of the medieval cloister, and its houses of brown sandstone stand beneath roofs consistently made of graded stone tiles, larger at the eaves than at the ridges. A fine stone bridge over the Derwent leads into the village from the south, and the village inn, the 'Lord Crewe Arms,' stands on the site of the former monastery's guest house. Blanchland is an inspired piece of modern village building which has fortunately protected itself from twentieth-century commercialisation, and long may it remain the unspoiled place it is.

Cambo and **Capheaton** lie not far apart on the other side of Hadrian's Wall. Both are model villages, as are so many in this county, but neither

Blanchland, Northumberland. This unique eighteenth-century village was built from the ruins of an abbey by the Bishop of Durham for the workers in his lead mines.

Wallington Hall. A mansion built by the Blackett and Trevelyan families who also built the model Northumberland village of Cambo. The grounds were laid out by Capability Brown.

has the faintest similarity to Blanchland except in being stone-built. Capheaton was largely built by the Swinburnes of Capheaton Hall, whose members included the poet Algernon Charles. Cambo was built chiefly by the Trevelyans of Wallington Hall, whose members included the historians Sir George and G. M. Trevelyan. Pauline Lady Trevelyan gathered about her the great artists and writers of her day, and important meetings took place between Swinburne and Ruskin, and between Millais and Ruskin's wife. Lord Macauley was related to the Trevelyans, and did some of his work here, as did Capability Brown, who was born at **Kirkharle**,

Bamburgh Castle, Northumberland. One of the mightiest fortifications of the north, largely rebuilt in modern times. Part of it was once a home for shipwrecked sailors.

educated at the school in Cambo village, and started his working life in the gardens at Wallington.

Elsdon was once a place of much importance, though it is now a quiet village in the moorlands with the Cheviot Hills rising beyond them. It was the capital of Redesdale, and had to withstand armed raids by red-haired Caledonian barbarians from the north through a long period of border warfare. The pele tower was the characteristic fortification in these parts for those people of standing who did not possess a castle, and many villages have the remains of one: Elsdon's belonged to the vicar. Pele towers were usually three storeys high, the windowless ground floor being a store-room where the owner's livestock might be secured in times of danger. Human occupants stayed higher up, hopefully out of harm's way. Elsdon is another village familiar with death on a large scale. A mass grave found here contained the bones of over 1000 men. They were soldiers killed in the Battle of Otterburn in 1388, familiar in border ballad as 'Chevy Chase'.

Etal and **Ford** are further examples of the model or estate village superimposed on a relatively empty landscape. Etal is a place of almost excessive tidiness, with rows of cream-painted houses, some stone-tiled and some thatched, between the manor house at one end of the street and, at the other, the ruins of a castle taken by the Scots in their successes before Flodden.

Ford's castle was taken at the same time, but this one was fully restored in the nineteenth century by Louisa, Marchioness of Waterford, who built the model village as a memorial to her Irish husband – known as the 'Mad Marquis' in hunting circles – who died after falling from a horse. Lady Waterford was a talented artist and a friend of Ruskin – a friendship that continued even after he saw her Biblical paintings on the walls of the village school. Ruskin told her in a letter of faint praise: 'I expected you would have done something better', after she had spent many years on the work, using the villagers as models – and keeping the younger ones happy with bread and jelly. Whether you like Ford village is a matter of taste. It is well designed and built, but totally foreign to this northern borderland of vast open spaces perfumed with the scent of wild roses, and looks more like a bit of nineteenth-century suburban Surrey.

Whittingham and **Holystone** are more natural-looking villages. The former has a pele tower which

Norham Castle, Sunrise. *Turner's famous painting is one of a long series he did of the border village's castle ruin over a period of forty years.*

later became an almshouse, and the latter has a holy well: a clear pool fed by a spring and surrounded by trees. The well is reached across a field behind the 'Salmon Inn', and has a cross standing in it and an old statue of Paulinus in the undergrowth nearby, for legend has it that the saint baptised 3000 local people at this spot in AD 627.

The red sandstone village of **Horncliffe** on the Tweed is England's most northerly village, but **Norham**, a little way upstream, is better known, as it contains the ruins of the border castle which gave Sir Walter Scott the starting point for his poem *Marmion*, and Turner the subject for a remarkable series of paintings, in which the castle perched on its cliff above the river is shown almost dissolved in hazy sunlight.

Even Turner would have been hard put to make the castle at **Bamburgh** seem like a melting vision. The huge and solid mass of this great coastal fortress totally dominates the village of grey stone at its foot,

and the biggest surprise here is that Bamburgh has managed to retain its village character round the triangular green, resisting the temptation to profit hugely from the tourists by turning itself into a popular resort. It is not only the castle that draws people to Bamburgh, however, for this village was the home of a famous English heroine, Grace Darling, who was born here in 1815, the daughter of the keeper of the Longstone Lighthouse on the Farne Islands. She persuaded her father to row out from the lighthouse with her in a terrible storm to rescue nine survivors from the ship *Forfarshire* wrecked in the gale, having seen them clinging to the rocks at dawn. She died of consumption four years later, when only twenty-seven years old, and was buried in the churchyard. The house where she was born is now the village post office, and there is a Grace Darling Museum where relics of the incident are preserved by the Royal National Lifeboat Institution.

Bewcastle, Cumbria. The seventh-century cross in the village churchyard, sadly deprived of its head, is one of the most amazing survivals of the Dark Ages in Europe.

THE NORTH-WEST

MERSEYSIDE and Greater Manchester have very little to offer village England, though even here the situation is not entirely hopeless. On the Wirral, for instance, is the country village of **Thornton Hough** with cottages, manor house, church and vicarage, village shop and smithy, a huge green and the open countryside beyond. This sounds like a delightfully unspoiled old place in an area few tourists head for, but in fact it is an estate village largely created by Lord Leverhulme – whose very different creation, Port Sunlight, is only a mile or two away – and it shows that the modern planned village need not be the soulless, uniform place foreign to the locality in which it is placed, that it so often is. The church clock of All Saints even has a nice touch of rustic eccentricity, with an extra clock face added to the

existing four because the previous landlord, Joseph Hirst, could not see the time from the windows of his house.

Lancashire, for all its large towns and industry, is a county where the old English village does survive intact, however. There is no space in this book to discuss all those industrial villages which now attract so much interest, but **Brindle** and **Tockholes**, standing on the very threshold of Blackburn, do deserve a mention. Brindle's Perpendicular church tower, from which Cromwell's troops are said to have fired on Royalist soldiers, looks uneasily across country today at the threatening approach of industry. Tockholes was a centre of the cottage weaving industry in 1662, when the Act of uniformity was passed making the revised

Thornton Hough, Merseyside. Formerly in Cheshire, this attractive model village is, as it were, the country cousin of Port Sunlight, built mostly by Viscount Leverhulme at the beginning of the century.

caused by the enclosure movement and against suppression of the religious houses. The abbot of Whalley, along with many other leaders of the march, was hanged for his part in it.

George Fox climbed Pendle Hill over a century afterwards: 'with difficulty, it was so very steep and high. When I was come to the top, I saw the sea bordering on Lancashire, and there ... the Lord let me see in what places He had a great people to be gathered.' The people of Lancashire were not always of the peaceful and contemplative kind embraced by Fox's Society of Friends, however, for they were deeply superstitious, and the villages around the whale-backed Pendle Hill were involved, only a few years before Fox came here, in the notorious episode of the Lancashire Witches. No English county persecuted so many poor village women more zealously than Lancashire, and on this hill the 'midnight hags' were popularly supposed to hold their covens. Twenty people were hanged in 1612 after witnesses swore on oath that the accused, among other evils, dug up corpses from graveyards. It is sobering to recall these incidents in **Downham** – one of the Pendle villages and now often called the prettiest in Lancashire – or wander among its brown stone cottages in their winding lanes, and watch ducks and young children innocently competing for paddling space in the little stream by the stone bridge. **Grindleton**, a long village below the hill in Ribblesdale, is said to have got its name from the fires kindled in local devil-worship.

Bolton-by-Bowland is a village of stone houses around two greens, at the edge of the upland area called Bowland Forest, and demonstrates, among other things, that characteristic Lancashire concern with outward appearances that other parts of the country might regard as tasteless fussiness, but which, in this corner, seems somehow as endearing as the habit of calling everybody 'love'. Here, the mortar between the stones is glaringly white. Elsewhere in the county, one sees lintels, window sills and other details painted in bright colours.

Slaidburn is a nice village, with an inn called 'Hark to Bounty'. This has nothing to do with Captain Bligh, however. Instead the name alludes to the vicar's dog, which was given what might be called benefit of clergy, when other local dogs were kept in order by whips which can still be seen in the church.

Inglewhite and **Goosnargh** are on the south side of the Forest not far off that rattling serpent, the

Liturgy compulsory in church services, and the parishioners here rebelled against this interference with their religious freedom and set a pattern of Nonconforming independence that recurs in Lancashire, not least at **Whalley**, which stands in a triangle with Blackburn and Burnley.

This large village has the remains of the Cistercian Whalley Abbey, which exercised great power and influence over a wide area before the Dissolution, and in 1537 its abbot supported the Pilgrimage of Grace, that essentially northern protest whose heralding beacons he had seen from Pendle Hill. It was a demonstration against rural hardship

Downham, Lancashire. Often called the county's prettiest village, it nestles nonchalantly beneath the sinister Pendle Hill, where Lancashire's notorious witches supposedly gathered.

M6 motorway, yet both seem far removed from the noise and industry of twentieth-century life. Inglewhite contains in its Button Row a former mill where buttons were made from bone, and Goosnargh has a manor house, Chingle Hall, which lays claim to the unenviable distinction of being the most haunted house in Britain. St John Wall was born here, and it is said that when he was executed for his faith, his severed head was brought back and secreted in the house, but the Franciscan monk is only one of the many ghosts which the imaginative have seen or heard here.

Hornby and **Gressingham** are on opposite banks of the River Lune. The former has a castle belonging to the local great family, the Stanleys, which stands high up and is visible for miles around; while the latter enjoys a nicely secluded position in the valley. Down-river is a well-wooded beauty spot called 'Crook of Lune', with the attractive village of **Aughton** nearby.

Across the M6 is the quiet resort of **Silverdale**, which the Victorian novelist Mrs Gaskell frequented, and inland are the lovely stone villages of **Yealand Conyers** and **Yealand Redmayne**. This trio completes a 'reet champion' picture of village Lancashire and brings us happily into Cumbria, where interesting and attractive villages are by no means confined to the Lake District.

Chingle Hall, Lancashire. The ill-fated manor house at Goosnargh is reputedly haunted by several ghosts, including that of St John Wall, who was born here.

Dent and **Ravenstonedale**, for instance, are Pennine villages, Dent being within the Yorkshire Dales National Park (although Yorkshire lost it to Cumbria in the recent boundary changes). Dent might be justifiably sensitive about being called a village. It was the former 'capital' of Dentdale and is still inclined to call itself Dent Town, for it was a self-contained community with its own local government made up of the property-owning farmers, called 'statesmen', in this region. A place of stone houses along narrow cobbled streets, it won itself an undeserved notoriety through its womenfolk, who supplemented the incomes of their farming or quarrying husbands by knitting garments from the coarse local worsted wool. It was Betty Yewdale, telling her story to the poet Robert Southey, who gave Dent its reputation. She was sent there with her sister to learn hand knitting when she was only seven years old and her sister five, and the lonely and frightened girls, far from their home in the Lake District, were overawed by the speed at which the local women could knit. 'They er terrible knitters e' Dent' Betty remarked, and the tag stuck. Betty and her sister 'teuk off' one dark night, wearing only their bedgowns and aprons, and trekked 25 miles

Dent, Cumbria. A village famous, or infamous, for its 'terrible knitters', it was also the birthplace of Adam Sedgwick, the pioneer geologist.

Slaidburn, Lancashire. The well-kept village in a valley below the Forest of Bowland used to be the region's administrative centre, and has a court room near the inn.

The 'Pepper Pot'. Lancashire is a county rich in 'follies',

and this one on Castlebarrow Head near Silverdale overlooks Morecambe Bay.

(40.2 km) back home through rain and snow. They never went back, but the 'terrible knitters of Dent' lived on in their memories until Southey published the story when Betty was an old woman.

Ravenstonedale is a grey limestone village of much style and character. It used to have a refuge bell in its old church, which was rebuilt in the eighteenth century, and any fugitive from justice who could reach the tower and toll the bell before his pursuers caught up with him was allowed to go free. The village inn with its mullioned windows is the 'Black Swan', but as the village name indicates, ravens were more common birds in these parts and, in fact, they menaced the livelihoods of the local farmers by swooping down from the lonely limestone crags to prey on weakling lambs. Up to the eighteenth century, two pence could be earned for every raven's head produced, but it must have been a hard-earned bounty.

The stream rippling through Ravenstonedale is the Scandal Beck, and it serves as a reminder that in this part of England the characteristically blunt, harsh words are a heritage of the long Viking occupation. The Viking influence is evident not only in the names of places but in the dialect and character of the people: 'beck', 'tarn', 'fell', 'scree', 'scar', 'gill' are Viking names. The Norsemen also left behind them a heritage of folklore peculiar to the region, such as its stronger belief than elsewhere in the 'little people', the elves and fairies, goblins and pixies. The seventeenth-century parish records at the hamlet of **Lamplugh**, near the Cumbrian coast, ascribe a death by drowning to being 'led into a horse-pond by a will o' the wisp', and three other fatalities as being 'frightened to death by fairies'.

The villages up the north eastern side of Cumbria usually feature much building in red sandstone, which is dressed into such small and smooth-faced blocks that it can be – and indeed is – mistaken for brick. It presents a very different village scene from

Patterdale, Cumbria. An attractive village at the head of Ullswater, built of neatly dressed Westmorland slate, and a popular centre for touring northern Lakeland.

the grey limestone of southern Cumbria and the slate of the Lake District. **Crosby Ravensworth** and **Temple Sowerby** show the contrast. The latter – in the valley of the River Eden – is often called the 'queen' of east Cumbrian villages. Crosby Ravensworth is a place of ancient occupation, for it has prehistoric circles and burial mounds all around it, and the remains of an extensive British settlement have been found nearby.

Dufton is another 'red' village, with a large green sporting a Georgian village pump which is painted maroon – a colour inexplicably popular in the Pennines, where it is frequently to be seen bringing a livid touch to doors, sills, lintels and such-like on barns as well as houses and cottages.

Long Meg and her Daughters. Workmen employed to destroy the Bronze Age stone circle near Little Salkeld fled in terror when a mighty thunderstorm blew up, and the circle remains.

Dufton, Cumbria. The Georgian pump on the village green is the purple patch in a Pennine story of red sandstone and green grass and trees.

Milburn should not be omitted from this account for the sake of prettier places, for it is a 'planned' village of a kind that may reflect the origin of all 'green' as opposed to 'street' villages (which often grew by ribbon development to take advantage of highway trade). Milburn is laid out on a rectangular plan with houses surrounding the green on all sides. Roads enter the rectangle at the corners and cross the green diagonally. The idea of this formation was that the village could virtually be 'closed' when raids threatened, keeping livestock safe on the green (a bit like a circle of covered wagons in Western films, but with Caledonian savages in place of Red Indian ones). The village school is well protected inside the rectangle, but not the church, for as Lord Melbourne once remarked: 'Things have come to a pretty pass when religion is allowed to invade the sphere of private life.'

Kirkoswald and **Great Salkeld** are villages that share an obvious Viking influence in their names and the ubiquitous red sandstone in their buildings. Kirkoswald has two knolls occupied by the ruined tower of a former castle and the detached bell tower of the parish church, which is 200 yards (180.2 m) away in a hollow. The tower must have been built on the hill so that the bell calling the faithful to worship could be heard in the farthest corners of the parish.

Near Great Salkeld is a more ancient place of worship – the stone circle known as Long Meg and Her Daughters, who were supposedly turned to stone for dancing on the Sabbath. Long Meg must have been a highly fertile female, but exactly how many daughters she had is a matter of dispute, for Wordsworth referred to 72 stones, Pevsner 59, and other accounts vary between these figures, one specifying 65 stones. In fact, legend has it that the stones cannot be counted accurately, but anyone who manages the trick will break the spell, and the stones will be transformed into village maidens before his very eyes.

Dancing girls or goddesses would doubtless have peered vainly at their reflections in Cumbria's jewelled mirrors if the Greeks, and not the Vikings, had inhabited the Lake District, perhaps residing on the mountain tops whose names would not have been so hard and unromantic as those we have inherited from the cold warriors of northern Europe – Scafell, Skiddaw, Pike of Blisco.

Across the M6 beyond Penrith is a beautiful part of England whose lakes, at least, are more lyrically christened. Approaching from this direction, the first lake is one of the biggest and best, Ullswater. It was on the west bank here that Wordsworth saw his daffodils, and he described the lake as 'upon the whole, the happiest combination of beauty and grandeur, which any of the Lakes affords.' The villages of **Dacre** and **Patterdale** sit at its northern and southern ends respectively. Dacre was the site of a monastery in the Anglo-Saxon period, where King Athelstan is supposed to have signed a treaty with the Scots, but it had no lasting effect, as can be seen by the number of pele towers built in the area.

Patterdale is an attractive village of stone buildings which is popular as a centre for walks along the lakeside, for climbing Helvellyn, and for taking steamer trips on the lake. What is particularly noteworthy in the village itself, however, among the more modern buildings, is the neatly dressed slate of which many houses are built. This is the first evidence of slate being used on a large scale encountered since Cornwall, and such usage continues through most of the Lake District villages, giving them often a coldish and sometimes slightly aggressive look, but wholly complementary to the landscape and unique in character.

Unless we are fell walkers, our move southward must be by the Kirkstone Pass, and this, the highest motor road in the district, brings us to **Troutbeck**, one of Lakeland's most fascinating villages, where slate lines the long village street in walls, cottages, barns and farmhouses. Once it was a string of separate hamlets on the road above Windermere, with groups of buildings situated near the ancient and precious wells which are dedicated to St Margaret, St James and St John. Troutbeck's

menfolk were either farmers or quarrymen, but it was noted at one time for breeding giants, who performed various feats of prodigious strength and wrought havoc among unwary Scottish raiders. One of them was Hugh Heard, to whom the king granted a tenement in the valley called Lowick How. It was said that Hugh had lifted a 30 foot (9.1 m) oak beam into position for a builder when 10 other men had failed to move it.

At the southern end of the village is Townhead, a typical 'statesmans' house owned by the National Trust, with the round chimneys characteristic of slate building – neat square corners being hard to achieve. Not far away are the remains of a farmhouse with a first floor spinning gallery, where the farmer's wife would have sat spinning the wool of the local Herdwick sheep. Troutbeck's hotel is called the 'Mortal Man', and has an inn sign which makes libellous allegations in verse about 'Sally Birkett's ale'. The village church is separate from the main community, standing in the valley below, and has stained-glass windows by William Morris and Burne-Jones.

In the central area of the Lake District enclosed by Windermere, Coniston Water, Grasmere and

Troutbeck, Cumbria. This attractive and fascinating slate village above Windermere is actually a string of former hamlets stretched out along one long road.

Elterwater, Cumbria. This village is a classic of vernacular building, with several cottages having huge shapeless slabs of slate as lintels and dressings, and all roofed with local slates.

Rydal Water is a cluster of villages which all seem characteristic of the region and yet display a great variety of style and situation. **Hawkshead** is a quaint and highly popular warren of narrow cobbled alleys and whitewashed cottages. The musem was once the grammar school attended by Wordsworth, and his desk can still be seen there with his name carved on it. Hawkshead looks like a typical Lake District village, yet only four miles away is the village of **Elterwater**, which is in total contrast to it but in some ways even more typical. This is a quarrying village, and its cottages of slate rubble proclaim a no-nonsense approach to a life which used to be hard in the extreme in this inhospitable region, where the quarries were usually high up on the fells, and men only came down to their homes at weekends, the journey on foot being too arduous to undertake every day. They came down on Saturday nights and left again before dawn on Monday mornings, often getting their brief relaxation from cock-fighting. There was a gunpowder factory at Elterwater, and during the week the mountains echoed with the thunder of explosions as great boulders of slate were detached from the host rock. Huge unshaped slabs of quarry waste were used as lintels and dressings for the houses in this fascinating village.

Grasmere, again, is a total contrast to both Hawkshead and Elterwater. This is a large village and exceptionally sedate by comparison, with Victorian houses and shops in a splendid setting, which attracts large numbers of summer visitors – it is a sort of northern Bourton-on-the-Water. What most of them come to see, of course, is Wordsworth's home, Dove Cottage, and the churchyard graves of the poet, his sister Dorothy, his wife Mary, their daughter Dora, and Coleridge's son Hartley, all together here with simple slate headstones. 'On Monday, 4 October 1802,' Dorothy wrote,

my Brother William was married to Mary Hutchinson. I slept a good deal of the night and rose fresh and well in the morning. At a little after eight o'clock I saw them go down the avenue towards the church. William had parted from me upstairs. I gave him the wedding ring – with how deep a blessing! I took it from my forefinger where I had worn it the whole of the night before – he slipped it again onto my finger and blessed me fervently.

Wordsworth, for all his daffodil fancying, was a rugged northerner in speech, manner and appearance – the painter Haydon described his head 'as if it was carved out of a mossy rock, created before the flood' – and he had none of the cultivated southern manners of Ruskin, the old man of **Coniston**, whose gravestone in that village churchyard is a much more elaborate and artistic affair.

More or less a contemporary of Ruskin's was Will Ritson, who kept the Wasdale Head Inn, and was an inveterate foe of urban airs and graces. The village

Coniston, Cumbria. A view across Coniston Water towards the quarrying village, with the much-plundered fell known as Coniston Old Man behind. It has yielded copper as well as slate.

Hawkshead, Cumbria. You could almost mistake it for a Cornish fishing village, with its old whitewashed stone buildings, archways and narrow streets, but it was a busy wool town once.

of **Wasdale Head** lies in a remote spot beyond the head of Wastwater, with Scafell and Great Gable towering over it, and an isolated churchyard containing the graves of climbers who lost their lives on the mountains. Wasdale Head has long been known for its claim to have England's highest mountain, its deepest lake, its smallest church and its biggest liar. It is wrong about the church, and if anyone ever overthrows its claim to have the biggest liar, he could substitute England's biggest rainfall, a fact which the villagers tend to keep quiet about. But so far, Will Ritson remains undisputed champion of the tall story, for centuries a favourite pastime of this region of long nights, possibly deriving, like so much here, from the sagas of the Vikings. Will Ritson would sit on a wooden bench in his back kitchen telling wildly far-fetched tales in his broad Cumberland dialect to eager and often gullible listeners; or accompany a visiting clergyman up Scafell and tell him at the top, with a distinct lack of reverence: 'Tha'll nivver be nighter t'heaven than noo'. Once he embarked on an epic tale, for the benefit of a group of women, about a family of eight who had been caught in a cloudburst on the fells, and who in their panic waded right into the raging water where, unable to help each other, they had all been swept away. His appalled listeners were lost for words, until Will broke the silence with, 'Ah weel, it might ha' been worse!' 'Worse?' gasped the dumbfounded women. 'Aye, it might ha' been true.'

Buttermere is a village between the lake of that name and Crummock Water, and is a good centre for walking this lovely countryside. It has a tiny church, and what is now the Fish Hotel was once the 'Char', where the Lake Poets, Wordsworth, Southey and Coleridge, were all drawn to set eyes upon the 'Buttermere Beauty'. This was not a rare species of butterfly, but the daughter of the innkeeper, who was renowned for her grace and modesty. But Mary Robinson was also naive, and she was married to a man who claimed to be an MP and the brother of an earl. Coleridge was instrumental in exposing him as an impostor. He was actually called Hatfield, and had a wife and family in Devon. He was well known in London as a swindler, and after leaving Mary pregnant, he made off. Hatfield was duly caught, tried and hanged for what the judge called a crime of 'such magnitude as has seldom, if ever, received any mitigation of capital punishment.' It was not rape or murder, nor even bigamy or adultery, but forgery, by which he had acquired 50 pounds.

Graves of the Wordsworth family. In St Oswald's churchyard at Grasmere are the simple headstones to 'old Wudswuth', as locals called the Poet Laureate, and his kin.

Two princesses figure among other Cumbrian village characters. The sandstone coastal village of **St Bees** is named after St Bega, an Irish princess who is said to have crossed the Irish Sea in a small boat to escape the unwonted attentions of a Norwegian prince, for she had vowed religiously to remain a virgin all her life. She won some land here from the local baron, Lord Egremont, and founded a nunnery, where the parish church now stands, with its spectacular Norman doorway.

The other princess is buried in the churchyard at **Finsthwaite**, a village near the southern end of Windermere. The white cross over her grave is inscribed to 'Clementina Johannes Sobiesky Douglass', and the identity of this lady, laid to rest here in May 1971, is among the unsolved mysteries of British history. At the foot of the cross are the words 'Behold thy king cometh', and it is believed that the lady was the daughter of Bonnie Prince Charlie, and thus might have become Queen of England in different circumstances. The 'Young Pretender' was the son of James Edward Stuart and Maria Clementina Sobieski, grand-daughter of John, King of Poland. Douglass was the incognito under which Charles Stuart travelled on the continent after his crushing defeat at Culloden. The lady buried here arrived in this village as a child in 1746 to live with a family of Catholics and Jacobite sympathisers named Taylor. The story is a complicated one, but this little known village certainly has the unique distinction of a guest claiming descent from both the Scottish and Polish royal lines.

St Bees, Cumbria. The spectacular Norman doorway of the village church, built of red sandstone on the site of a nunnery founded around 650 AD.

Rivalling Bonnie Prince Charlie in fame is John Peel, whose grave is in **Caldbeck**, on the northern fringes of the Lake District. If Will Ritson's irresistible talk recalls Dolly Pentreath of far-away Cornwall, John Peel's fame in ballad is reminiscent of Tom Cobleigh in distant Devon, for the song written about Peel by his friend John Graves is known throughout the world, and it became the

Caldbeck, Cumbria. The grave of John Peel, the irrepressible huntsman made immortal by the ballad written by his friend John Woodcock Graves in 1832.

march of the Border Regiment after the Charge of the Light Brigade at Balaclava, when the infantrymen whistled the tune as they helped the cavalry prepare for the attack. Peel was born in this village in 1776, the son of a horse-dealer, and all his life hunted the fox, mainly on foot on the fells, with his 'coat so grey' woven from the local wool in its natural colour.

Beyond Carlisle and the Roman wall, almost at the northernmost tip of Cumbria below the slopes of the Cheviot Hills, is a hamlet called **Bewcastle**, and here our tour of English villages comes to an end. From Barfrestone in Kent to Bewcastle in Cumbria might not seem to have got us very far in terms of an A–Z of English villages, but as far as the huge variety and fascinating contrasts of this country are concerned, there could hardly be two more illuminating representatives, and between them is an untold wealth for which this book can only be, at best, a sampler or appetiser.

Bewcastle's church, though largely rebuilt, was originally of the thirteenth century, and is dedicated to that famous northern saint, Cuthbert, the Bishop of Lindisfarne, but the village itself is much older than either, and it may stand as a symbol of the growth of English villages through all the ages. The Romans had a fort here as an outpost of the wall, and no doubt a small civilian settlement grew up in its shadows, supplying labourers for the Empire, consumer goods for the officers, prostitutes for the troops. When the Angles came, they erected a cross here, in the seventh century, richly carved with Runic inscriptions and Coptic devices, within the Roman fortification whose stone went into the building of the expanding village. This monolith is a shaft of light from the Dark Ages – a 1300 years-old work of art in local sandstone, unrivalled in Europe, which survived the Viking hordes, the centuries of border warfare when several pele towers were built in the vicinity, and the ravages of wind and storm. It was only in relatively modern times, when the antiquary William Camden took an interest in it, that its decay began, for its head was sent to Camden for study and never came back.

This exquisite but broken column stands as a symbol of village desecration, and the moral is clear. If English villages are to survive the onslaught of industry, over-population and tourist traffic, we must all protect and defend them even as we enjoy their rich variety and fascination, and the dangers are hardly less in the secluded corners of northern England than in the traffic-devastated countryside of Kent. It is our duty to those who come after us, for as H. Rider Haggard, himself a rural Englishman, wrote not too long ago:

In this twentieth-century England we seem to have grown away from the land; we have flocked into cities; we have set our hearts on trade, and look to its profits for our luxury. But the land is still the true mother of our race, which, were it not for that same land, would soon dwindle into littleness.

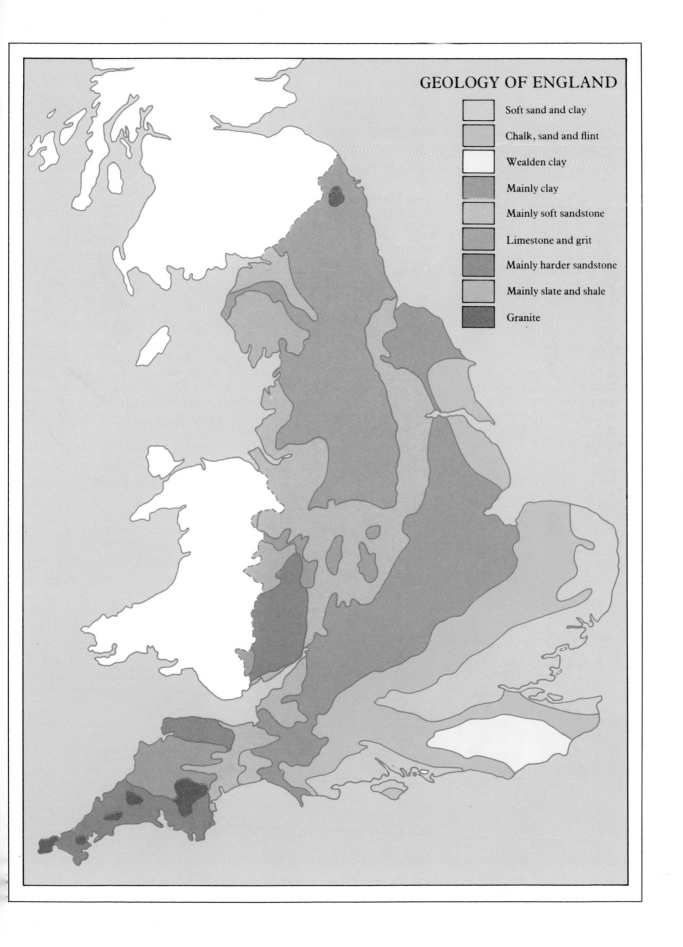

GEOLOGY OF ENGLAND

Soft sand and clay

Chalk, sand and flint

Wealden clay

Mainly clay

Mainly soft sandstone

Limestone and grit

Mainly harder sandstone

Mainly slate and shale

Granite

ACKNOWLEDGMENTS

The author and publishers would like to thank the following for supplying photographs for reproduction:

Malcolm Aird: 17 right, 34 bottom
Brian Bailey: 74 top and bottom, 76 bottom, 146
Rita Bailey: 34 top
John Barrow: 7
John Bethell: 52, 62, 72, 80, 88, 114
Janet and Colin Bord: 10 bottom, 11, 14 top, 15 top and bottom, 24, 29 bottom, 40 bottom, 41, 45 left, 59 top and bottom, 60, 63, 64, 65 bottom, 73, 78, 79 left, 79 right, 85 top and bottom, 92, 97, 102 left, 106, 107, 108, 109, 115, 116, 119, 144, 145
Cambridge University Aerial Survey: 105 top
Eastern Daily Press: 93 top
Mary Evans Picture Library: 9, 27 top, 35, 61, 121 left
Fotobank/English Tourist Board: 77, 83, 122, 123, 131, 133
Fotobank: 48–9 (Andy Williams), 70–1 (Patrick Wise), 82 and 103 (Jeffrey Whitelaw)
Hove Library: 6
A.F.Kersting: endpapers, frontispiece, 8, 12, 14 bottom, 22, 30, 38, 47, 55, 57 bottom, 69, 100–1, 105 bottom, 117, 126, 130
S.& O.Mathews: 13, 17 left, 18, 51, 56 bottom, 86 bottom, 91, 113
Cressida Pemberton-Pigott: 134, 140
Peter Phillips: 43, 65 top, 94, 104
Kenneth Scowen: 20–1, 23, 27 bottom, 28, 32, 33, 42 top and bottom, 44 top, 45 right, 56 top, 57 top, 71 top, 75, 81, 87, 98, 99, 102 right, 121 bottom, 124, 135 top, 141
Edwin Smith: 36 top and bottom, 39, 58, 67
Swanston Graphics: 10, 26, 40, 54, 68, 84, 100, 116, 132, 147
Tate Gallery: 86 top, 129
Towner Art Gallery: 16
Trustees of Stanley Spencer: 66 (Tate Gallery)
Derek Widdicombe: 31 top and bottom, 37, 44 bottom, 46, 53, 76 top, 89, 93 bottom, 96 (Noel Habgood), 110–1, 112, 118, 120, 121 right (Noel Habgood), 125, 128 (Noel Habgood), 135 bottom, 136–7, 138, 139, 143 bottom
Stuart Windsor: 19, 50 top, 148
Trevor Wood: copyright page, 25, 29 top, 43, 65 top, 90, 94, 95, 104, 142, 143
George Wright: 50 bottom

Effigy of Alice, Duchess of Suffolk, on her tomb at Ewelme, Oxfordshire.

INDEX OF VILLAGES

GENERAL INDEX